THE BLACK-SCHOLES AND BEYOND INTERACTIVE TOOLKIT

A Step-by-Step Guide to In-Depth Option
Pricing Models

THE BLACK-SCHOLES AND BEYOND INTERACTIVE TOOLKIT

A Step-by-Step Guide to In-Depth Option Pricing Models

NEIL A. CHRISS

MCGRAW-HILL

New York   San Francisco   Washington, D.C.   Auckland   Bogotá
Caracas   Lisbon   London   Madrid   Mexico City   Milan
Montreal   New Delhi   San Juan   Singapore
Sydney   Tokyo   Toronto

Library of Congress Cataloging-in-Publication Data

Chriss, Neil, 1997
    The Black-Scholes and beyond interactive toolkit : a step-by-step
guide to in-depth option pricing models / Neil A. Chriss.
      p.   cm.
    Toolkit associated with: The Black-Scholes and beyond / Neil A.
Chriss. 1997.
    Includes index.
    ISBN 0-7863-1026-X
    1. Options (Finance)—Prices—Mathematical models.   2. MATLAB.
I. Chriss, Neil, 1967– Black-Scholes and beyond. II. Title.
HG6024.A3C494   1997
332.63'228—dc21   96–40002

McGraw-Hill

A Division of The McGraw·Hill Companies

2 3 4 5 6 7 8 8 9 DOC/DOC 9 0 9 8 7

ISBN 0-7863-1026-X

Printed and bound by R. R. Donnelley & Sons Company.

This publication and the accompanying software are designed to provide accurate and authoritative information in regard to the subject matter covered. It is sold with the understanding that neither the author or the publisher is engaged in rendering legal, accounting, or other professional service. If legal advice or other expert assistance is required, the services of a competent professional person should be sought.
        —From a Declaration of Principles jointly adopted by a committee
        of the American Bar Association and a Committee of Publishers.

This publication and the accompanying software are provided for educational purposes only. In option trading there can be no assurance of profit. Losses can and do occur. As with any investment, you should carefully consider your suitability to trade options and your ability to bear the financial risk of substantial losses. Do not assume that theories, systems, methods, or indicators presented herein will be profitable or that they will not result in losses. The accompanying software produces options prices using information available to the public. No representation is made that the prices produced by this software are accurate or that the software itself is free of defects.

McGraw-Hill books are available at special quantity discounts to use as premiums and sales promotions, or for use in corporate training programs. For more information, please write to the Director of Special Sales, McGraw-Hill, 11 West 19th Street, New York, NY 10011. Or contact your local bookstore.

INSTALLATION INSTRUCTIONS AND SYSTEM REQUIREMENTS FOR THE IBM PC

WHAT IS THE *BLACK-SCHOLES AND BEYOND INTERACTIVE TOOLKIT*?

The *Interactive Toolkit* consists of this book and a diskette containing four software programs for an IBM PC or Compatible machine.[1] The software is full color point and click software consisting of:

- An options pricing calculator;
- A hedging game that simulates hedging six types of options in a variety of markets; and
- Two tools for studying random numbers and probability distributions.

The software is fully loadable on any PC meeting the minimum requirements below and does not need any other software to run. It is intended to be used with this book as an aid to learning options pricing. If you require a Mac version of the software, please call 630-789-5516. Leave your name, address, and phone number; a copy will be sent promptly.

System Requirements

The *Black-Scholes and Beyond Interactive Toolkit* requires:

- MS Windows 3.1 or Windows 95 on a 386, 486, or Pentium system.
- Math coprocessor chip.
- High density 3-1/2 inch floppy disk drive.
- MS Windows-support monitor (8-bit graphics recommended).
- At least 8MB of RAM, and 6 megabytes of available disk space.

Installation Instructions

1. Insert the *Toolkit* diskette into your floppy disk drive.
2. *a.* From the Windows Program Manager, pull down the **File** menu and select the **Run...** option.
   b. Or from the Windows 95 task bar, choose **Start** and select **Run.**

---

[1]Macintosh Version is available; contact the publisher for details.

3. At the **Command Line** prompt, type *a:setup* (or *b:setup*) and click **OK.**

4. At the **Installation Location** prompt, enter the name of the directory into which you want to install the *Black-Scholes and Beyond Interactive Toolkit.* The default directory is *BSBEYOND.* Click **OK.**

5. Insert diskette **2** when prompted. When installation is complete, click **OK.**

6. After installation is complete, double click on the MATLAB icon to start the *Black-Scholes and Beyond Interactive Toolkit.*

CONTENTS

Introduction

What Is MATLAB? 1

Chapter 1

Put-Call Parity in Option Pricing 7

Chapter 2

Probability Theory 17

Chapter 3

The Black-Scholes Formula 23

Chapter 4

Black-Scholes and Lumpy Dividends 31

Chapter 5

Options on Futures—Black's Models 35

Chapter 6

Hedge Parameters for European Options and the Black-Scholes Formula 39

Chapter 7

Options on Currencies Using the Black-Scholes Formula 51

Chapter 8

Black-Scholes Implied Volatility 55

Chapter 9

The Construction of Binomial Trees 63

Chapter 10

Pricing Options on Binomial Trees 75

Chapter 11

Implied Volatility Trees 87

Chapter 12

Pricing Barrier Options   107

Chapter 13

Pricing Barrier Options in the Presence of the Smile   125

Chapter 14

Studying Options through Simulated Hedging   129

Appendix A

Using *Black-Scholes and Beyond Interactive Toolkit* Software   141

Appendix B

Using the *Black-Scholes and Beyond Interactive Toolkit* with the Options Calculator   149

Appendix C

Using the MATLAB Command Window   151

THE BLACK-SCHOLES AND BEYOND INTERACTIVE TOOLKIT

A Step-by-Step Guide to In-Depth Option Pricing Models

⑥ INTRODUCTION

Congratulations! You have just purchased a great way to learn about options pricing. With the *Black-Scholes and Beyond Interactive Toolkit,* you will have state-of-the-art options pricing models at your fingertips. You will be able to explore the option pricing models in *Black-Scholes and Beyond* with an easy-to-use, graphical user interface that makes options pricing easy. Here are just a few examples of what you will be able to do with the Interactive Toolkit:

- Calculate option prices using the Black-Scholes formula, Cox-Ross-Rubinstein trees, equal probability trees, or Derman-Kani implied volatility trees.
- Enter in today's volatility smile, graph it in three dimensions, view it from all angles, and then build an implied volatility tree.
- Build binomial trees, price options on them, and then display the various option pricing trees, such as the stock price tree, the option pricing tree, the Arrow-Debreu price tree, and the local volatility tree.
- Take any binomial tree and graph its terminal probability distribution.
- Compute all types of barrier option prices and their greeks using Cox-Ross-Rubinstein, equal probability, or implied volatility trees.
- Graph in two or three dimensions any option price or hedge parameter for a variety of options against any input parameter for any option pricing model. For example, you can "see" the relationships between interest rates, volatility, and the delta of a barrier option.

The *Interactive Toolkit* uses the state-of-the-art MATLAB™ numerical computational and graphics tool as a backend for these models.

EXERCISES TO GO WITH THE TOOLKIT

The *Interactive Toolkit* comes with an elaborate set of exercises to guide you through the models in *Black-Scholes and Beyond*—from the most basic of concepts through the most complex ideas. The *Toolkit* was designed to be a teaching tool as well as a full-fledged options pricing calculator. As a result, there are many features not ordinarily available in option pricing calculators, such as the ability to view binomial trees produced by the calculator. For example, you can price an American option, and then, with the press of a button, you can view the option price tree and see where the early exercise boundary is.

As another example, in *Black-Scholes and Beyond* you learned that the enhanced binomial method (*Black-Scholes and Beyond,* pp. 467–473) improves the convergence of pricing barrier options on a binomial tree. With the *Interactive Toolkit* you will be able to graph barrier options prices against the number of periods in the binomial tree and compare the unenhanced and enhanced methods. You will be able to put both graphs (enhanced and unenhanced) right next to each other and see the difference for yourself.

The *Interactive Toolkit* will be useful for anyone who wants to price options using today's option pricing models, as well as anyone who wants to learn option pricing in a hands-on way. There's even more, though!

A HEDGING GAME

The *Interactive Toolkit* comes with a special bonus: a hedging simulation. This "game" allows you to sell one of six types of options to a client (European and American, barrier and vanilla) and then hedge the option using a variety of strategies. Your "control screen" contains all the information an options trader has at his desk: a calculator that instantly tells you your option values and greeks, the current market for the stock, and your current position. You get graphs of stock price and historical volatility, and you have to decide how to hedge the option. Your guide is the analytics provided by the built-in options pricing calculator. Here are some additional features of the game:

1. As you trade, your profits and losses are tallied, and you can introduce a credit limit.

2. You get to choose the trading environment. You trade in the Black-Scholes world of constant volatility and interest rates and no transaction costs, or you can introduce any of the following extra conditions:

    a. *Black-Scholes world with unknown volatility.* You will learn that even if we do live in a constant volatility world, historical volatility does not look constant, and it is difficult to decide the correct volatility with which to hedge.

    b. *Bid-ask spread.* You can vary stock price liquidity from 100% (no bid-ask spread) down to very choppy markets with large spreads. See how your profits and losses diminish as liquidity decreases.

    c. *Stochastic volatility.* You can introduce random volatility into your trading world. You choose the amount of correlation between stock price and volatility, and you choose between mean reverting and ordinary stochastic volatility.

    d. *Jumps.* In *Black-Scholes and Beyond,* we learned that stock price jumps ruin the Black-Scholes hedging strategy. Now try for yourself to hedge when stock prices jump.

INTRODUCTION TO THE TOOLKIT

The *Black-Scholes and Beyond Interactive Toolkit* is divided into chapters that loosely correspond to topics covered in the main text, *Black-Scholes and Beyond.* You do not need to have read *Black-Scholes and Beyond* to use the *Toolkit;* any basic grounding in options pricing theory will do. The purpose of the *Toolkit* is to allow the user to explore the ideas in *Black-Scholes and Beyond* in depth in a hands-on way. The tools for this exploration are the software packages included with the *Toolkit,* and your guide to exploration is this book. Most of the chapters are divided into several parts as follows:

1. Review of concepts.
2. Computer tutorial.
3. Questions for basic understanding (in some sections).
4. Review questions.

We discuss each section in detail.

Review of Concepts

Review material serves as a basic reintroduction to the topics in the text. In some cases, however, this book goes beyond *Black-Scholes and Beyond* and introduces new material. In such cases, the review material is a quick introduction to the subject; in these cases, we believe the material is easily understood by anyone grasping the basics of option pricing.

Computer Tutorial

The *Black-Scholes and Beyond Interactive Toolkit* software is easy to use, but each section includes a computer tutorial as a quick way of learning how to use the relevant parts of the computer programs available to you. These sections discuss only the material relevant to the section at hand, and, as such, each section of the book becomes independent of the others. You can pick up the book in the middle and quickly get started on any chapter.

REFERENCES TO *BLACK-SCHOLES AND BEYOND*

In many places in this book we refer to *Black-Scholes and Beyond;* if you do not already own this book, it is a good companion to have while using the *Black-Scholes and Beyond Interactive Toolkit.* All references to *Black-Scholes and Beyond* refer to Neil A. Chriss, *Black-Scholes and Beyond* (Burr Ridge, IL: Irwin Professional Publishing, 1996).

ACKNOWLEDGMENTS

This book was written while I was working in the Institutional Equity Derivatives department at Morgan Stanley and Company. I would like to thank Fred Bird and Peter Carr (Morgan Stanley) for some interesting conversations. I am especially indebted to Marcus Hancock (Smith Barney) for a great deal of advice on the Options Calculator and the hedging game.

The Mathworks Inc. was crucial in making this project a success. I would like to thank Chris Garvin for a great deal of technical assistance, Cathy de Young and Mike Wolf for their efforts in making the whole project possible, and Sean Curry for his enthusiasm and support of the project.

⑥   WHAT IS MATLAB?

The *Black-Scholes and Beyond Interactive Toolkit* Options Calculator and SimuHedge were created using MATLAB™. When you run the Options Calculator and SimuHcdgc, you are running a demonstration version of MATLAB compiled especially for Irwin Professional Publishing by The Mathworks Inc. The full version of MATLAB is available from The Mathworks on a variety of platforms. You do not need to own MATLAB to use the Toolkit.

MATLAB™ for Finance is a complete financial modeling, research, and application development environment, featuring breathtaking graphics, a compiler/code generator, spreadsheet links, and more than 25 toolboxes that add advanced specialized tools in various domains (e.g., finance, optimization, statistics, and neural networks).

Educators, students, quantitative analysts, portfolio managers, and other finance practitioners use MATLAB to analyze risk, optimize portfolios, and evaluate hedging strategies. The power and flexibility of MATLAB lets each user reflect his or her individual view of markets and methodologies through the analytical methods that user prefers. Only MATLAB integrates accurate, high-performance computation with advanced visualization in an open, standards-based environment.

As an open system, MATLAB runs on all the most popular desktop and server platforms, and functions developed on one platform run on any other without modification. MATLAB's open architecture also offers application-specific extensions ranging from highly advanced technologies (wavelets, neural networks, and dynamic simulation) to core financial techniques such as statistical analysis and optimization.

MATLAB's unique Handle Graphics™ architecture supports both sophisticated data visualization and the development of robust graphical user interfaces to MATLAB-based applications. Because all of these functions coexist in the same integrated environment, every step in the application development process from prototyping to testing to production can be accomplished smoothly and easily. The MATLAB Financial Toolbox also includes finance-specific graphic formats such as logarithmic scales, hi-lo, candlestick, and Bollinger bands.

MATLAB also features a compiler/code generator that supports standard ANSI C on all platforms and has an external interface library that provides both integration of legacy code and increased performance for speed-critical functions. A C Math Library lets developers use the MATLAB computational facilities from standalone programs that run outside the MATLAB environment. Spreadsheet interfaces to Excel (under Windows) and Applixware (under UNIX) provide an additional platform application development and deployment as well as data presentation and preprocessing.

These benefits and others too numerous to list here have led to widespread adoption of MATLAB in both commercial and educational applications. For more information, visit the MATLAB for Finance website at http://finprod.mathworks.com. To obtain more information about The Mathworks, please call 508-647-7000.[1]

---

[1]The author and Irwin Professional Publishing are not in any way compensated for the preceding information about The Mathworks.

1

⑥ PUT-CALL PARITY IN OPTION PRICING

REVIEW OF MAIN CONCEPTS

Put-call parity is the relationship between European put prices and European call prices of the same strike and expiration. If C and P are a put and a call on the same underlying S, then the basic formula is:

$$C(K, T) - P(K, T) = S - e^{-r(T-t)}K,$$

where S is the stock price, K is the strike price, T is the expiration date, and t is the current time. Here $C(K, T)$ represents the value of a call on S expiring at time T and struck at K, and likewise, $P(K, T)$ is the put value.

When the stock pays dividends, the situation is slightly different. Let $(D_1, t_1), (D_2, t_2), \ldots, (D_n, t_n)$ be dividend payments and ex-dividend dates of all the dividends with ex-dividend dates between now and the expiration of the option. Let D be the present value of all the dividends payments in the schedule. Then we have *put-call parity with dividends:*

$$C(K, T) - P(K, T) = S - Ke^{-r(T-t)} - D.$$

COMPUTER TUTORIAL

Start by loading the options pricing calculator:

- Load the Toolkit mainscreen.
- Move the mouse button over the choice "Options Calculator," and press the left mouse button.

A screen should appear with the title "Black-Scholes and Beyond Toolkit: Options Calculator."

To do the questions in this section you will need to know how to

- Use the Black-Scholes formula to price a call or put option.
- Graph option values versus interest rates.
- Adjust the values of the various input parameters to the Black-Scholes formula.

We now discuss these points.

Valuing Options Using the Interactive Toolkit Options Calculator

1. Choose an underlying security. Select the desired type of underlying from the "Underlying Type" menu. Move the mouse pointer to the "Underlying Type" menu, put it directly over the name of the underlying type, and click the left mouse button. Select the underlying of choice by dragging the mouse to the desired underlying and releasing the button. The name of your selected underlying should appear.

2. Choose an option type. Move the mouse over the "Option Type" menu, and press the left mouse button while the pointer is over the name of the option type (e.g., Vanilla Call). A menu should pop up with a list of option types. Drag the pointer to the name of the option type you wish (in this section, Vanilla Call or Vanilla Put) and release. The option type name should change to the desired type.

3. Choose a value for each input parameter. There are sliders for each of the input parameters S (stock price), K (strike price), r (risk-free rate), σ (volatility) and T (time to expiry). The dividend value (q) may also be changed by adjusting the slider labeled "Dividend Rate." Here is a summary of the input variables and the appropriate slider. This chart is valid when the underlying type label reads "Stock or Index."

Parameter Name	Symbol	Slider Label
Stock price	S	Stock Price
Strike price	K	Strike Price
Risk-free rate	r	Interest Rate (%)
Volatility	σ	Volatility (%)
Time to expiry	T	Expiry (...)
Dividend yield	q	Dividend Yield (%)

4. Enter a dividend schedule (optional). To enter a dividend schedule, press the pushbutton ENTER DIV'DS located in the lower left part of the calculator:

    a. *Choose the number of ex-dividend dates or clear.* A screen will appear asking you the number of ex-dividend dates to enter. The box will initially display a number. You may do one of two things:

        i. Change the value in the display box and press OK. This will bring you to the next screen.

        ii. Press CLEAR. This will clear the current set of dividends in the system, set all dividends to zero, and put you back in the main option calculator.

b. *Enter the dividend payments and ex-dates.* After you press OK, a second screen will appear labeled "Black-Scholes and Beyond Toolkit: Dividend Entry." There will be two rows of numbers:

i. Top row, ex-dividend date. The ex-dividend date is entered based on the amount of time from today. It is measured in the same units as you have chosen in the "Expiry (Units)" submenu of the "Configuration" on the Options Calculator screen. The Dividend Entry screen will say at the top how time is measured. For example, if time is currently measured in days then the top of the screen will read:

Ex-div date in Days from Today.

When you pull up the screen, a list of possible ex-dividend dates will already be given on the screen. You may change these dates to anything you want. To do so, move the mouse pointer to the date you want to change, and click on the box. This will put a cursor inside of the box. You may edit the box this way.

ii. Bottom row, dividend payment. Enter the dividend payment in the box below the ex-dividend date.

c. *Press ACCEPT to enter the dividends.* When you are done entering the dividends, press the ACCEPT button. This will enter the dividend into the system. The next time you bring up the Enter Dividends screen, this is what you will see.

d. *Press QUIT to erase the current entry.* If you press QUIT, the screen will close, and everything you entered will go away. The set of ex-dividend dates and times present in the system *before* you brought up the Enter Dividends screen will remain in the system. Next to Expiry will be the current units the expiry is in, e.g., "Expiry (days)" or "Expiry (years)." Use the slider to adjust the value of the desired parameter.

e. If you press the left slider, the value will decrease; if you press the right slider the value will increase.

f. The slider moves values at discrete intervals. For more precise intervals, enter the number directly by moving the pointer over the value display (to the right of the parameter name) and clicking the left mouse button. A cursor should appear, and you can then enter the number. When you are done, you can hit RETURN or do nothing. The number will be registered when you value the option.

5. Change to desired time units. Time to expiry can be in days, weeks, months, or years. To change expiry units to solve a problem, move the mouse pointer to the menu bar item labeled "Configuration." Click the left button. Drag the pointer over the item labeled "Expiry (units)." A second menu will appear with the items Days, Weeks, Months, Years. Move the pointer over the item of your choice and release.

6. Select the evaluation method. You may select one of a variety of choices for how to evaluate the option. In this section you will only evaluate vanilla options, so choose one of three methods:

a. *Select Analytic for Black-Scholes.* To evaluate options with the Black-Scholes formula, set the evaluation method to analytical. In this case, only European options will be evaluated.

b. *Use a tree method for American options.* If you wish to also value American options (which you will be asked to do below), select a binomial tree method:

i. Select Binomial: CRR for Cox-Ross-Rubinstein trees. If you want to evaluate on a Cox-Ross-Rubinstein tree, select this option.

ii. Select Binomial: Equal Prob for Equal Probability trees. If you want to evaluate on an Equal Probability tree, select this option.

Once you have selected a binomial tree, a slider display will appear with the number of time periods on which to evaluate the tree. You may select any number of periods between 1 and 100. For additional periods, proceed as follows:

i. Pull down the "Configuration" menu.

ii. Go to the "Periods Max" menu, and select "Min = 100, Max = 500."

7. Value the option. Move the pointer to EVALUATE OPTION, and press the left mouse button.

a. If the evaluation method is analytic, the option value will appear in the box labeled European Value. The box labeled American Value will display the letters N/A for Not Applicable because the Black-Scholes method is only for European options.

b. If the evaluation method is a tree method, both the European option value and the American option value will be displayed.

8. Be aware.... When you press EVALUATE OPTION, the option calculator reads the current state of all the sliders and menus and makes the calculation based on that state. If, after the calculator finishes, you change some values, the option value displayed will no longer correspond to the input parameters displayed.

9. View the dividends after you have entered the dates. You may view the dividends currently in the system at any time after you have entered the dividends. If there are non-zero dividends in the system, a button will appear in the Options Calculator screen labeled VIEW DIV'DS. If you press the button, the following information will be displayed:

a. *All dividends and ex-dividend dates.* The same display for entering dividends will reappear. Note: You may at this time alter the dividend dates or payments.

b. *The present value of all dividend payments occurring before the current expiry.* When you press VIEW DIV'DS, the options calculator looks at the value in the Expiry slider and computes the present value of all dividend payments that occur before this date. This value is displayed in a box in the upper right corner of the dividend display, labeled PV OF DIV'DS.

Graph Option Values in Two Dimensions

1. Choose an item for the X-axis. Move the mouse pointer to the menu labeled "X-Axis" and choose an appropriate parameter for the X-axis. The menu will display the following list:

Underlying
Strike
Barrier
Expiry (...)
Risk-free rate (%)
Volatility (%)
Periods

The choice "Barrier" is the barrier level for input options and is thus irrelevant for vanilla options. The choice "Periods" refers to the number of periods in a binomial tree and thus is irrelevant for the Black-Scholes formula. If you choose either of these you will get an error screen.

2. Choose an item for the Z-Axis. Because we allow graphing in three dimensions, we call the vertical graphing axis the Z-axis. Here is a list of valid items for the vertical axis:

Option value

Option delta

Option gamma

Option theta

Option vega

Option rho

3. Choose an option type. To graph vanilla call options, set the "Option Type" menu to Vanilla Call. To graph vanilla put options, set the "Option Type" menu to Vanilla Put.

4. Choose a valuation method. In this section we will use the Black-Scholes formula, so set the options valuation method to Analytic.

5. Set the input parameters. You have already chosen a variable for the X-axis. This means the other input variables are fixed. For example, if you want to graph stock price on the X-axis and option values on the Z-axis, you will want to choose values for r, σ, T, K and q. To do so, simply set the appropriate sliders as in the previous section on evaluation options.

6. Graph the option. To graph the option, press PLOT X-Z. An option graph screen will appear with the graph you requested.

7. Keep the screen up as long as you like. When you are done viewing the option graph, you may kill the screen by moving the mouse over the QUIT button in the bottom right corner of the screen, or you may leave the screen up and make another graph. For example, you might want to make two graphs with stock price in the X-axis, but with put value in one case and call value in the other.

8. Keep in mind.... When you press PLOT X-Z, the options calculator reads all of the relevant sliders and makes a plot based on those input parameters.

QUESTIONS FOR BASIC UNDERSTANDING

1. Set the input parameters as follows:

$$S = 100$$
$$K = 100$$
$$r = 5\%$$
$$q = 0\%$$
$$\sigma = 30\%$$
$$T = 1 \text{ year}$$

Now make the following computations:

a. Compute the value of a vanilla European call with the preceding input parameters [i.e., compute $C(S, T)$].

b. Compute the value of a vanilla European put with the preceding input parameters [i.e., compute $P(S, T)$].

c. Using a calculator compute

$$C(S, T) - P(S, T)$$

d. Using a calculator compute

$$S - e^{-rT}K$$

e. If you did everything correctly, you should find that put-call parity holds. That is, you should find that

$$C(S, T) - P(S, T) = S - e^{-rT}K$$

plus or minus one penny (the one penny is due to rounding of option prices).

2. Now leave all parameters the same, but change the volatility to 15%. That is, the parameters should now read

$$S = 100$$
$$K = 100$$
$$r = 5\%$$
$$q = 0\%$$
$$\sigma = 15\%$$
$$T = 1 \text{ year}$$

Now repeat the steps in question 1:

a. Compute the value of a vanilla European call with the preceding input parameters [i.e., compute $C(S, T)$].

b. Compute the value of a vanilla European put with the preceding input parameters [i.e., compute $P(S, T)$].

c. Using a calculator compute

$$C(S, T) - P(S, T)$$

d. Using a calculator compute

$$S - e^{-rT}K$$

Note: The right side of the equation

$$C(S, T) - P(S, T) = S - e^{-rT}K$$

did not change. This is because S and K do not depend on the value of σ. Despite this, each of $C(S, T)$ and $P(S, T)$ changed. Conclusion: Although each of $C(S, T)$ and $P(S, T)$ changed, their difference $C(S, T) - P(S, T)$ did not change.

3. Put call-parity with dividends. Enter the following dividend schedule into the system:

$$T_1 = 1/2 \text{ year}$$
$$D_1 = \$1$$

$T_2 = 1$ year
$D_2 = \$1$

Keep the parameters set as listed:

$S = 100$
$K = 100$
$r = 5\%$
$q = 0\%$
$\sigma = 15\%$
$T = 1$ year

Now we will verify put-call parity with dividends.

    a. First compute $C(K, T)$ and $P(K, T)$ and finally

$$C(K, T) - P(K, T)$$

    b. Now compute the present value of the dividend payments, D, by pressing the VIEW DIV'DS button.

    c. Compute

$$S - e^{-rT}K - D$$

    d. Verify that

$$C(K, T) - P(K, T) = S - e^{-rT}K - D$$

to within 1 penny accuracy.

REVIEW QUESTIONS

Answer the following review questions using the Options Calculator to aid your intuition.

    1. Let $T = 1$ be one year from today, $r = 5\%$, $q = 0$, $\sigma = 15\%$, $S = \$100$ and $K = \$100$. Suppose $P(100, 1)$ is trading at $\$3$. What is the value of $C(100, 1)$?

Continuing with the previous question, use the Options Calculator to make a graph of the value of interest rates versus the value of $C(100, 1)$.

    2. Note that as the risk-free rate rises, the call value rises as well. What is the intuitive explanation for this? (Hint: As the interest rates rise, the forward value of a stock rises as well.)

    3. Repeat the previous question, but graph the vanilla put value versus interest rates instead. What is the relationship between the European put value and interest rates? Why is this relationship different than that of a European call option?

    4. This exercise explores the following question: Does put-call parity depend on the future stock price distribution of S? To answer this, proceed as follows:

    a. Choose values for σ, r, K, $T - t$, and S, and compute the Black-Scholes value for a call and a put based on these values. Compute $C(K, T) - P(K, T)$, and verify that it is equal to $S - e^{-r(T-t)}K$.

    b. Do not change your initial choice of r, K, $T - t$, or S. Now compute $C(K, S)$ and $P(K, S)$ for a variety of values of σ. If you make no mistakes in your computation, the individual values of $C(K, S)$ will change as the volatility changes, but the difference $C(K, T) - P(K, T)$ will not change. The conclusion is that while put and call prices are dependent on volatility, the value $C(S, T) - P(S, T)$ is not.

    c. Now look back at the derivation of put-call parity (see *Black-Scholes and Beyond*, p. 40–43), and explain why put-call parity does not depend on the stock price distribution.

    5. Recall the following fact: An American option on a nondividend paying stock is never exercised early by a rational investor (see *Black-Scholes and Beyond*, pp. 45-48). On the other hand, we have seen that an American option on a nondividend paying stock will sometimes be exercised. Fix values for S, t, T, K, σ, and r, and use the Options Calculator to compute the following values, assuming the stock does not pay dividends:

$$C_{am}(T, K) \qquad C_{eu}(T, K) \qquad P_{am}(T, K) \qquad P_{eu}(T, K),$$

where C_{am} means American option price and C_{eu} means European option price.

    If you have calculated correctly, the European and American call prices will be the same, but the American put price will be greater than the European put. Now compute:

$$C_{am}(T, K) - P_{am}(T, K)$$
$$S - e^{-r(T-t)}K$$

Describe the differences in the sets of values. If the first line were equal to the second line, we would have put-call parity. Describe why the first value is smaller than the second value. (see *Black-Scholes and Beyond*, p. 47) What does this say about the arbitrage argument in put-call parity? Now use the computer to help answer the following questions:

    a. If you vary T, K, r, or S, is it possible that $C_{am}(T, K) - P_{am}(T, K)$ could be greater than $S - e^{-r(T-t)}K$? Explain in terms of arbitrage (see BSB p.45).

    b. Using the computer, try to convince yourself that the following inequalities always hold:

$$S - K < C_{am}(T, K) - P_{am}(T, K) < S - Ke^{-r(T-t)}.$$

    6. Prove put-call parity with dividends using an arbitrage argument.

    7. Let $S = 100, K = 100, \sigma = 15\%$, and $r = 5\%$. Let t be today and T be one year from today. Moreover, suppose the stock will have two ex-dividend dates in the next year: the first, one month from now, will pay \$1.00, and the second, seven months from now, will pay \$0.50. If $P(K, T)$ is trading at \$3.00, what is the value of the corresponding call?

    8. Use put-call parity to derive a general rule for when the price of a European put is greater than the price of a European call when the put and the call have the same underlying, time to expiry, and strike price.

Solutions

Problem 1
To answer this question, we use the put-call parity equation directly, which in this case reads:

$$C(100, 1) - P(100, 1) = S - e^{-r \cdot T}K.$$

In this equation we know the values of $P(100, 1)$, S, K, r and T. Substituting these values we obtain:

$$C(100, 1) - 3 = 100 - e^{-0.05 \cdot 1} 100.$$

Using this we find immediately that $C(100, 1) = 7.8771$. Note that we did not use the volatility in this computation. This is because the right-hand side of the put-call parity equation does not depend on volatility.

Problem 2

It is an interesting fact that as the risk-free rate of interest rises, so does the value of a European call option. Let's explore why. When the risk-free rate rises, the forward value of a stock rises too. This is due to the arbitrage relationship between the stock price and its forward value (see *Black-Scholes and Beyond, p. 48*). Put another way, the cost of locking in the future cost of a stock increases with the risk-free rate of interest. Now, buying an option is nothing more than buying participation in the upside of a stock's movement.

2

⑥ PROBABILITY THEORY

REVIEW OF MAIN CONCEPTS

A random event or variable is a mathematical description of "something that happens." It describes the possible outcomes of the event and the probability of each outcome (when there are a discrete set of outcomes) or the probability of any range of outcomes (when there are a continuous set of outcomes).

Sampling from a Distribution: Histograms

A sample from a probability distribution is simply a number. Taken by itself, it has little meaning, but repeated sampling from a distribution gives it meaning. For example, consider the random variable described by the flip of a fair coin: There is a 50% probability of heads (call it 1) and a 50% probability of tails (call it -1). A sample from this distribution is nothing more than one of the numbers $+1$ or -1. This in itself tells us nothing. But 1,000 samples from this distribution will have approximately 500 $+1$'s and 500 -1's.

A *histogram* graphically displays the results of multiple samples from a distribution. Suppose we take 1,000 samples from a normal distribution. If we simply make a list of the numbers, they won't appear to have much structure. For example, what follow are 50 samples from a normal probability distribution with mean 0 and standard deviation 1:

Samples

0.8476	0.3750	−1.0982	−0.5077	1.1330
0.2681	1.1252	1.1226	0.8853	0.1500
−0.9235	0.7286	0.5817	−0.2481	0.7031
−0.0705	−2.3775	−0.2714	−0.7262	−0.0524
0.1479	−0.2738	0.4142	−0.4450	2.0185
−0.5571	−0.3229	−0.9778	−0.6129	0.9242
−0.3367	0.3180	−1.0215	−0.2091	−1.8141
0.4152	−0.5112	0.3177	0.5621	0.0350
1.5578	−0.0020	1.5161	−1.0639	−1.8079
−2.4443	1.6065	0.7494	0.3516	1.0282

FIGURE 1

A Histogram of 50 Numbers

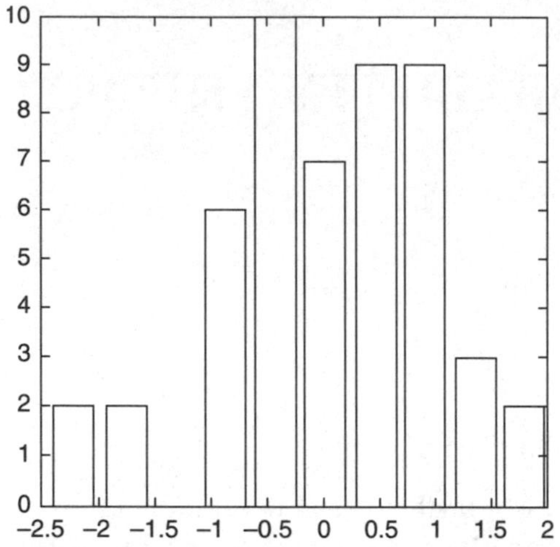

Figure 1 displays the same data in a histogram. Each tower of the histogram represents the number of samples in the range given by the base of the tower. The height of the tower represents the number of samples in that range.

The Normal Distribution Function

The normal probability distribution is defined by the probability density function

$$\frac{1}{\sigma \sqrt{2\pi}} e^{-(x-\mu)^2/2\sigma^2},$$

where μ is the mean of the distribution and σ is the standard deviation.

If X is a normal distribution of mean μ and standard deviation σ, then the *standard* normal distribution Φ is given by

$$\Phi = \frac{X - \mu}{\sigma} \tag{1}$$

A sample from a normal distribution X is a number produced randomly in such a way that its probability of falling into a given range is given by X. The *cumulative normal distribution function* of X gives the probability that for a given number x, a sample from X is less than or equal to x. Given Φ, the standard normal distribution, then we write $N(\cdot)$ for the *standard* cumulative normal distribution function; that is,

$$N(x) = Pr(y \leq x),$$

where y is a sample from a standard normal distribution.

COMPUTER TUTORIAL

The *Black-Scholes and Beyond Interactive Toolkit* comes equipped with two tools to help you learn about probability theory:

1. The Distribution Tool.

2. The Random Number Tool.

Both of these tools have been provided to the *Black-Scholes and Beyond Interactive Toolkit* by The Mathworks Inc. and are part of the MATLAB statistics toolbox.

What follows is a summary of the Distribution Tool and the Random Number Tool.

The Distribution Tool

The Distribution Tool allows you to look at a variety of probability density functions and their cumulative normal distribution functions. Here is a detailed list of the functionality:

- A graph of the cumulative normal distribution (cdf) function or probability distribution function (pdf) for a given distribution and set of parameters.
- A pop-up menu for changing the distribution function, this chapter deals exclusively with the Normal distribution.
- A pop-up menu for changing the function type (cdf or pdf).
- Sliders to change parameter settings.
- Data entry boxes to choose specific parameter values.
- Data entry boxes to change the limits of the parameter sliders.
- Draggable horizontal and vertical reference lines to perform interactive evaluation of the function at varying values.
- A data entry box to evaluate the function at a specific *x* value.
- For cumulative normal distribution plots, a data entry box on the probability axis (Y-axis) to find the critical value corresponding to a specific probability.
- A CLOSE button to end the session.

Example   To plot the normal distribution function with mean 0 and standard deviation 1, do as follows:

1. Set the distribution pop-up to *Normal*.

2. Set the function type pop-up to *PDF* (probability distribution function).

3. Set the *Mu* slider to 0.

4. Set the *Sigma* slider to 1.

The Random Number Tool

The Random Number Tool allows you to sample from a variety of distributions and build histograms. The tool provides a way to choose a probability distribution, set its parameters, sample from the distribution, and display the sample in a histogram.

Here is a list of the features of the Random Number Tool:

1. A histogram of the sample.
2. A pop-up menu for changing the distribution function.
3. Sliders to change the parameter settings.
4. A data entry box to choose the sample size.
5. Data entry boxes to choose specific parameter values.
6. Data entry boxes to change the limits of the parameter sliders.
7. A **RESAMPLE** button to allow repetitive sampling with constant sample size and fixed parameters.
8. A CLOSE button to end the demonstration.

Example   To draw 1,000 samples from the normal distribution with mean 0 and standard deviation 1, proceed as follows:

1. Set the distribution pop-up menu to *Normal.*
2. Set *Mu* to 0.
3. Set *Sigma* to 1.
4. Set the *Samples* box to 1,000.
5. Press the RESAMPLE button.

Pressing the RESAMPLE button will draw 1,000 samples and then draw a histogram of the result.

REVIEW QUESTIONS

1. Use the Random Number Tool to draw 100 samples from a normal distribution with mean 0 and standard deviation 1 and produce a histogram (see *Black-Scholes and Beyond,* pp. 82–84). Now repeat the experiment with 500, 1,000, and 10,000 samples. What is the shape of the histogram? Now plot a normal probability density function (using the Distribution Tool) with mean 0 and standard deviation 1, and compare it with the histograms. Describe how the histogram relates to the normal distribution.

2. Use the Random Number Tool to sample from a normal distribution with mean 0 and standard deviation 3. First make a histogram with 100 samples, then 1,000, and finally 5,000. What are the maximum and minimum values of the sample? Repeat the experiment with a standard deviation of 8. What are the new maximum and minimum values? Explain.

3. Assume we have a normal distribution X with mean μ and standard deviation σ different than 0 and 1 (choose μ and σ now). Now choose a number x. Use the same sampling method as described earlier to approximate the probability that a sample from X is less than some number x. Now use equation (1) and the standard cumulative normal distribution function to compute the same probability. How does your answer compare?

The Normal Distribution and Geometric Brownian Motion of Stock Price Movements
Use the Distribution Tool to help answer the following questions.

4. Suppose a stock S is trading today at $100, and it follows a geometric Brownian motion (see *Black-Scholes and Beyond*, pp. 93–116) with instantaneous drift $\mu = 5\%$ per annum and volatility $\sigma = 15\%$ per annum.

a. What is the probability that in one year stock price will be greater than $110? $120? $150?

b. What is the probability that the stock price will be less than $90?

c. What is the probability that the stock price will be between $104 and $106?

d. Now assume that volatility of the stock doubles to 30%, and recompute the answers to parts a, b, and c. What happens to the probabilities? Explain your answers.

e. Now assume the volatility of the stock is only 1%, and recompute your answers to parts a, b, and c.

5. Verify the statement in the quote by Jackwerth and Rubinstein on page 116 of *Black-Scholes and Beyond*.

6. A digital call option pays $1.00 if the stock price is greater than K at expiration and $0.00 otherwise. If a stock currently trading at $100 follows a geometric Brownian motion with $\mu = 10\%$ and $\sigma = 20\%$, what is the value of the following digital options:

a. A two-week digital call option with strike $100. Repeat with $105.

b. A six-month digital call with strike $100.

c. A one-year digital call with strike $100.

d. Repeat the question with $\sigma = 40\%$. What happens to the prices? What is the intuitive explanation?

Solutions

Problem 1

As the number of samples increase the shape of the histogram looks increasingly like the normal distribution curve. The histogram is nothing more than a plot of relative frequency of the samples and where they appear. Why do they fall into place and look like a normal distribution? The answer lies in the connection between the normal density function, the normal distribution, and the definition of probability.

To understand this, suppose we make a histogram by hand. We start by drawing 10 bins (see *Black-Scholes and Beyond*, p. 82) spaced equally around zero and .05 apart. For example, there is a bin that will contain all samples for 0 and up to but not including .05. Suppose our first sample is .0135. This number will go in the bin we just mentioned. What was the probability of this happening? The probability is given by the area under the normal density curve between 0 and .05 (see *Black-Scholes and Beyond*, p. 85). If we keep drawing from the normal distribution, the bins will fill up with a relative frequency equal to the probability given by the normal curve. Now, since the heights of the bars of the histogram display the relative frequency, which is the probability of occurrence, the shape of the histogram naturally mimics the shape of the normal curve.

Problem 2

As the standard deviation of a normal distribution widens, so does the dispersion of values around the mean (see *Black-Scholes and Beyond,* p. 76). This means that the wider the dispersion, the less likely a particular sample will fall near the mean. When we sample from a distribution, the samples will naturally reflect this fact. As we see when we histogram the normal distribution, the maximum and minimum values of the distribution with standard deviation three are much closer to the mean than in the case of eight. This is a graphical demonstration of that mathematical fact.

3

⑥ THE BLACK-SCHOLES FORMULA

REVIEW OF CONCEPTS

The Black-Scholes option pricing formula has the following input variables:

S = stock price
K = strike price
r = risk-free rate of interest (per annum)
σ = volatility of the stock (per annum)
T = time until expiration (in years)
q = continuous dividend yield (per annum)

We assume the stock follows a geometric Brownian motion; the formulas for puts and calls are as follows:

$$C = N(d_1)Se^{-qT} - e^{-rT}N(d_2)K$$

$$P = -N(-d_1)Se^{-qT} + e^{-rT}N(-d_2)K$$

where

$$d_1 = \frac{\log(S/K) + (r - q + \sigma^2/2)T}{\sigma\sqrt{T}}$$

$$d_2 = d_1 - \sigma\sqrt{T}$$

Sometimes we write

$$C(S, K, T, r, \sigma, T)$$

$$P(S, K, T, r, \sigma, T)$$

to indicate the dependence of the option value on its input parameters.

COMPUTER TUTORIAL

In this section we are concerned with pricing European call and put options on a stock or index. To use the *Black-Scholes and Beyond Interactive Toolkit* to do this, use the following steps:

1. Basic setup
   a. Set "Option Type" to Vanilla Call, Vanilla Put, or Butterfly Spread.
   b. Set "Evaluation Method" to Analytic.
   c. Set "Underlying Type" to Stock or Index.
2. Set parameters
   a. Set Stock Price slider display to desired stock price.
   b. Set Strike Price slider display to desired strike price.
   c. *For butterfly spread only:* set the upper and lower strike slider displays. A butterfly spread is a combination of three options with three different strikes, K_1 (lower strike), K_2 (upper strike), and K (middle strike).
   d. Set Interest Rate slider display to desired risk-free rate.
   e. Set Volatility slider display to desired volatility.
   f. Set Div'd Yield slider display to desired dividend yield.
   g. Set Expiry slider display to desired expiry.
   h. Options
      i. *Changing expiry units.* To change the expiry units to a different unit of time (e.g., days instead of years), pull down the "Configuration" menu and the submenu Expiry (Units), and select a new set of units.
      ii. *Changing graph resolution.* You may change the resolution of all graphs produced by the toolkit from Course to Normal to Fine. To do so, pull down the "Configuration" menu and the submenu Graph Resolution, and select the resolution of your choice.
      iii. *Changing the output precision.* You have a choice between output precision of two or four digits. To change the precision pull down the "Configuration" menu and the submenu Output Precision. Choose between two and four digits.
      iv. *Changing the maximum slider value.* Sliders have maximum values so that their values slide smoothly. To change the maximum of a slider, pull down the "Configuration" menu:

      • To change Stock or Strike, use the Stock submenu (the two have the same maximum).
      • To change Interest Rate or Dividend max, use the Risk-Free Rate submenu.
      • To change Volatility max, use the Volatility submenu.

      v. *Changing the days in a year.* You may change the number of days used in days-in-a-year computation to 365 (default), 250, or 360. To do this, pull down the "Configuration" menu and use the Days in Year submenu.
3. Price the option: Once all parameters have been selected, click the EVALUATE OPTION pushbutton. The price of the option will be displayed in the European Value display box.

Graphing Option Values

To graph the value of an option proceed as follows:

1. Choose the type of option to evaluate from the "Option Type" menu.
2. Choose the method of evaluation from the "Evaluation Method" menu.
3. Choose the type of underlying from the "Underlying Type" menu.
   a. Choose a value for the X-axis. Pull down the X-axis menu, and choose value to vary for the X-axis.
   b. Choose a value for the Y-axis (three-dimensional plotting only). Pull down the X-axis menu, and choose a value to vary for the X-axis.
   c. Choose a value for the Z-axis. Pull down the Z-axis menu, and choose a value for the Z-axis (vertical axis) of the graph. To plot the option value, choose Plot Option.
   d. To plot in two dimensions, click PLOT X-Z.
   e. To plot in three dimensions, click PLOT X-Y-Z.
   f. To zoom in on the graph (two-dimensional graphs only), you may either "draw" the portion of the graph you want to enlarge by holding down the left mouse button, or simply click the left mouse button on any portion of the graph you wish to enlarge. To zoom out, click the right mouse button on a portion of the graph.
   g. To rotate the graph (three-dimensional graphs only), hold down the left mouse button over any portion of the graph. A framed box will appear. Move the box to the desired orientation and release the left mouse button. To move the box correctly, the X on the box must be toward its bottom.

REVIEW QUESTIONS

In the first set of questions choose values for K, T, r, and σ that will not change throughout. Compute the following set of questions as a unit.

    1. Choose a value of S so that a European vanilla call option is in-the-money. Calculate the Black-Scholes value of the call option. Now change the stock price so that the option is twice as much in-the-money (e.g., if $K = 100$ and $S = 105$, then change S to 110). Compute the option value with the new stock price. By what percent did the option's value increase?

    2. Choose a value of S so that a vanilla call option is out-of-the-money as it was in-the-money in the previous question. Calculate the Black-Scholes value of the option. Now change S so that the option is twice as much out-of-the-money (e.g., if $K = 100$ and $S = 95$, change S to 90). Compute the option's value with the new stock price. By what percent did the option's value decrease?

    3. Account for the differences in the percent changes in questions 1 and 2. Why did the option price almost double in the first question but not almost halve in the second?

    4. To build your intuition from the previous question, make a graph of stock price versus option value as follows:

- Set stock price to $100.
- Set strike price to $100.

- Choose any numbers you wish for T, σ, and r.
- Plot underlying versus option value.

Examine the graph. The horizontal (X-axis) can be divided into three regions: out-of-the-money, near-the-money, and in-the-money. The option value graph is virtually flat in the out-of-the-money region, curved in the near-the-money region, and linear (i.e., it is a line), in the out-of-the-money region. Answer the following questions:

    a. Intuitively what is the reason that the graph is flat in the out-of-the-money region?

    b. What is the reason the graph is linear in the in-the-money region?

    c. What do you think the slope of the linear portion of the graph is?

    d. How do these questions relate to the previous question?

  5. Set

$$S = 100$$
$$K = 0$$
$$\sigma = 15\%$$
$$r = 5\%$$
$$T = 1 \text{ year}$$
$$q = 0$$

    Do the following:

    a. Compute the value of a European call and a European put on the stock. The value should be equal to the current value of the stock. Why?

    b. Graph the option value versus risk-free rate. What does the graph look like? Why?

    c. Graph the option value versus volatility? What does the graph look like? Why?

    In the next set of questions you will make specific computations to learn about option values. Set

$$S = 100$$
$$K = 100$$
$$\sigma = 15\%$$
$$r = 5\%$$
$$T = 1 \text{ year}$$
$$q = 0$$

  6. Compute the Black-Scholes call price and Black-Scholes put price. Write down your answers for future reference. Does put-call parity hold?

  7. Suppose we double the volatility so that $\sigma = 30\%$ but leave the values of all the other parameters constant. Compute the new put option price. What value of S will make the call option value equal to the value when the volatility was 15 %? Record your answer for future reference.

  8. Set $\sigma = 7.5\%$, and leave the other parameters as given. Compute the new call option price. What value of S will make the call option value equal to the value when the volatility was 15 %?

9. Can you deduce any general principles about the relationship between call option value, volatility, and stock price? (To aid your intuition, make a graph of volatility versus option price when $S = 100$ and $K = 100$.)

10. Repeat questions 7, 8, and 9 using interest rates instead of volatility.

11. Now return all the parameters to their preceding values, but set $T = 6$ months. Compute the Black-Scholes call value. Double the volatility to 30 %, and recompute the option value. Did the value increase by as much as when there was one year to expiration? Put another way, is the option more sensitive or less sensitive to volatility changes at six months to expiration or one year to expiration?

12. Repeat question 11 using interest rates instead of volatility.

13. Return the parameters to the ones given earlier, and change the time to expiration to two weeks; recompute the Black-Scholes call value. Now change the time to expiration to one week (thus halving the time to expiration). Recompute the Black-Scholes call value. Record your answer for future reference.

14. In going from one year to six months to expiration, by what percentage did the option value change? In going from two weeks to one week to expiration, by what percentage did the option value change? Can you explain the difference?

15. Return the parameters to their previous values, but increase the dividend yield to 3%. What happens to the value of the option (does it increase or decrease)? Explain intuitively (see *Black-Scholes and Beyond,* p. 161–162).

16. Repeat the same question with a put option. Do you think the put option value will behave the same as with the call?

17. Return the parameters to their previous values, but set $q = 1$ % and $r = 4$ %. Compute the Black-Scholes call value. Is this the same as for $r = 5$ % and $q = 0$ %. Is this what you expected?

An option is *at-the-money forward* if its strike price is equal to its forward price at expiration, that is, if

$$K = e^{-Tr}S$$

where

$K = $ strike price
$S = $ stock price
$r = $ risk-free interest rate
$T = $ time to expiry

Write F for the forward price of the stock. The following is an approximate formula for the value of an at-the-money forward call option based on the Black-Scholes formula:

$$C = \frac{1}{\sqrt{2\pi}} \sigma \sqrt{T} e^{-rT}$$

where π is the numerical constant approximately equal to 3.14159265.

18. Set

$$S = 100$$
$$K = 100$$
$$r = 0\%$$
$$\sigma = 10\%$$
$$q = 0\%$$

Make a two-dimensional graph of volatility versus option value. Is the line a straight line? What is the slope of the line?

19. Confirm or disprove the formula for the call option value for the set of parameters given by using the Options Calculator.

20. Try to derive a similar formula for put options. (Hint: Can you use put-call parity?) Confirm your formula using the Options Calculator.

Option Sensitivities 1

In the next set of questions you will use option values or graphs to try to answer some questions about the general properties of option values. Some of the questions are answered in the text of *Black-Scholes and Beyond,* but try to use the Options Calculator to come to your own conclusions.

21. Make a graph of interest rates (of the underlying) versus Black-Scholes call option value. What happens as interest rates increase? Do you think the *moneyness* of the option plays a role?

    a. If the option is deep in-the-money, is it still sensitive to interest rates?

    b. If the option is deep out-of-the-money, is it sensitive to interest rates?

    c. When do you think the option's value will be most sensitive to interest rates?

    d. Deduce, using put-call parity, the answers to the same questions for vanilla European put options.

22. Make a graph of volatility (of the underlying) versus Black-Scholes call value for an at-the-money call. What does the graph look like? How could you make use of this information? If we change the option to deep in-the-money, do you think the option will be more or less sensitive to volatility? At what moneyness do you think the option will be most sensitive to changes in volatility?

23. Make a graph of time to expiration versus Black-Scholes put value. When is the option most sensitive to changes in time? Theta is also called time decay. What about the graph suggests this name? Make several graphs and try to determine for what moneyness the option is most sensitive to time changes.

24. For a given option (European call or put) (i.e., for a given time to expiration, strike price, and stock price), does the option become more or less sensitive to time changes as volatility increases?

25. For a given time to expiration, does increasing volatility of the underlying always increase option value?

26. Suppose we have a European call option on some stock. If the stock price, the strike price, the risk-free rate, and volatility of the underlying stay the same, will the option value always be less one day later? Is the same true for a put option?

Solutions

Problems 1, 2, and 3

To tackle these questions, we will use the options calculator to make a chart of option value versus strike price for options with 30 days to expire, with $\sigma = 15\%$, $q = 0\%$, $r = 10\%$.

			Stock price		
	90	95	100	105	110
Values	$0.02	$0.35	$2.15	$6.01	$10.83

When the stock moves in price from $100 to $105, the option value increases from $2.15 to $6.01, an almost threefold increase in value. When the stock price increases from $105 to $110 option value rises to $10.83, an almost doubling in value. What this shows is that the gearing percentage sensitivity of the option value decreases as the option moves more into the money. When the option is deep in the money, it behaves essentially like the underlying. A dollar rise in the value of the underlying produces a dollar rise in the value of the option. Despite this, the percentage changes work quite differently. As we saw above a move from at-the-money to 5 % in-the-money tripled the option value. This is an example of the leveraged nature of option prices, and why they are both profitable and dangerous. An option is said to be a leveraged derivative instrument because it magnifies changes in its underlying. The more the magnification, the more leveraged the instrument is.

If you have a view that a stock price will rise 5 %, what is the best way to profit from this view? Clearly an at-the-money option allows you to "do more" than investing in the equity itself. Of course, there is a danger in this view: If the option expires out of the money, you lose your entire investment.

On the other hand, when the option moves from at-the-money to out-of-the-money, the option value drops extremely rapidly. A 5% drop in stock value results in a drop in option value from $2.15 to $0.35, a drop to one-sixth its original value. The drop in stock price from $95 to $90 produces an even more dramatic drop in option value.

Given the above, use the options calculation to answer the following questions: What effect do the following have on an options leverage on its underlying's price:

1. volatility
2. interest rates
3. time to expiry

4

⑥ BLACK-SCHOLES AND LUMPY DIVIDENDS

REVIEW OF CONCEPTS

A dividend schedule is a list of dividend payments and ex-dividend dates:

$$(t_1, D_1), \ldots, (t_n, D_n)$$

Given an option with parameters:

$$
\begin{aligned}
S &= \text{stock price} \\
K &= \text{strike price} \\
\sigma &= \text{volatility per annum} \\
r &= \text{risk-free rate of interest per annum} \\
T - t &= \text{time to expiration}
\end{aligned}
$$

We assume the ex-dividend dates all occur between t and T (otherwise, we eliminate the ones that do not). We construct the present value (with the risk-free rate) of all dividends in the schedule

$$D = \sum D_i e^{-r(T-t_i)}$$

We form a new value

$$S^* = S_0 - D$$

and a new volatility

$$\sigma^* = \frac{S_0}{S*}\sigma$$

The Black-Scholes values of a vanilla European call C with the preceding parameters and a vanilla European put P with the preceding parameters are given by the following extension of the Black-Scholes formula:

$$C = S^*N(d_1) - e^{-r(T-t_0)}N(d_2)K$$

$$P = -S^*N(-d_1) + e^{-r(T-t_0)}N(-d_2)K$$

$$d_1 = \frac{\log(S^*/K) + (r + (\sigma^*)^2/2)(T-t)}{\sigma^*\sqrt{T-t}}$$

$$d_2 = d_1 - \sigma^*\sqrt{T-t}$$

COMPUTER TUTORIAL

To use the Black-Scholes formula to value options on a stock with lumpy dividends, proceed as follows:

1. Create a dividend schedule:

$$(t_1, D_1), (t_2, D_2), \ldots, (t_k, D_k)$$

2. Enter the dividends into the system:

a. Click the ENTER DIV'DS button

b. Enter the number of dividends payments into the box labeled "Number of Dates." For example, if there are eight dividends payments in your dividend schedule, enter 8 dividends.

c. Click OK to enter the dividend schedule. If you do not wish to click OK, you may do one of two things:

i. Click QUIT. This will close the screen; you will return to the main screen, and nothing will change with the system.

ii. Click CLEAR. This will clear all of the dividends from the system.

3. Enter the dividend schedule. After you press OK, a new screen will appear with a list of ex-dates and payments.

a. The top row of boxes represents the ex-dates. Enter the ex-dates in the same units as the expiry. For example, if your Expiry slider display reads "Days," then enter your list of ex-dividend dates in days from today.

b. The bottom row represents dividend payments. Enter the dividend payments in dollars.

4. Finish entering your schedule. When you are done entering the schedule, click ACCEPT to enter the dividends into the system or QUIT to erase the currently entered dividend schedule. If you QUIT, the dividend schedule that was in the system prior to entering your data will remain.

5. Evaluate options. Once you enter a dividend schedule into the system, all subsequent option evaluations will assume your underlying has this dividend schedule.

6. View or change the dividends. If there are dividends currently in the system, a button will appear.

REVIEW QUESTIONS

In the following questions, all calls and puts, unless otherwise stated, are vanilla European puts.

1. For a call option on a given stock, does increasing total dividend payments over the life of the option increase or decrease the value of the option? Repeat the question for a put. Explain intuitively.

2. Repeat the previous question (question 1), for a put option. Confirm your answer in a similar manner to the model answer above, and then use put-call parity with dividends (see Chapter 1 of this book) to attack the question from a different angle.

3. Consider the parameter values

$$S = \$100$$
$$K = \$100$$
$$\sigma = 15\%$$
$$r = 5\%$$
$$T - t = 1 \text{ year}$$

and the dividend schedule

$$(0.2, \$.50); (0.3, \$.75); (0.4, \$1.00)$$

where 0.2 means "two-tenths of a year from today," 0.3 means "three-tenths of a year from today," etc. Use the Black-Scholes formula to compute the value of a vanilla European option on S with the given parameters.

4. Convert the preceding dividend schedule to a continuous annual dividend yield q by solving the following equation for q:

$$S - D = e^{-q(T-t)}S$$

Now recompute the value of the option using the Black-Scholes formula with continuous dividends, and compare it with the value computed with lumpy dividends.

5. Add the following to the dividend schedule of S:

$$(0.1, \$.50); (0.25, \$.50); (0.35, \$.50); (0.45, \$0.50)$$

Repeat questions 2 and 3. First value the call option on S using lumpy dividends. Next convert the lumpy dividend to a continuous dividend yield, and compute the option value using the Black-Scholes formula with dividends. Did the approximation improve as compared with the smaller dividend schedule? Explain intuitively. (Note: The intuition behind this is similar to that of compound interest, see *Black-Scholes and Beyond,* pp. 57–60.)

Solutions

Problem 1

To answer this question, let's first use the calculator to guide us.

We will value a European call option on a stock with the following input parameters:

$$S = 100$$
$$K = 100$$
$$T = 1 \text{ year}$$
$$r = 10\%$$
$$\sigma = 15\%$$

and a single dividend payment 1/2 a year from today. The Black-Scholes value of this European call option is $10.99. Now let's increase the dividend payment to $2, and re-evaluate the option. The new value is $10.34. Thus the value of the option has decreased. Let's see why intuitively.

From the main text of *Black-Scholes and Beyond* (see pp. 154–162) we have seen that buying an option on a stock with lumpy dividends is much like purchasing an option on a stock whose value is reduced by the present value of the dividends. For this reason, the option on the stock with a greater total dividend stream is "more" out-of-the-money, and therefore worth less.

5

⑥ OPTIONS ON FUTURES— BLACK'S MODELS

REVIEW OF CONCEPTS

The topic of options on futures is a new topic and is not covered in *Black-Scholes and Beyond*. Nevertheless, the concepts are quite simple and can easily be understood.[1]

Let S be some security (e.g., a stock index), and let F be the futures price of the asset with delivery date T (current time equal to t). Let C be a vanilla European call option on F that expires at time T^*; similarly, let P be a vanilla European put option on F that expires at time T. Let K be the strike price, and let σ be the volatility of S. Recall the meaning of the call option: If the option is exercised at time T^*, the holder takes possession of a long position in a futures contract at time T^* with delivery T (for this reason, we assume that T^* is before T, i.e., $T^* < T$).

Assume that the volatility of S is constant throughout the life of the option. Then we have

$$C = e^{-r(T^*-t)}(FN(d_1) - KN(d_2))$$

$$P = e^{-r(T^*-t)}(-FN(-d_1) + KN(d_2))$$

where

$$d_1 = \frac{\log(F/K) + \frac{\sigma^2}{2}(T^* - t)}{\sigma\sqrt{T^* - t}}$$

---

[1]The formulas found in this chapter were originally derived in F. Black, "The Pricing of Commodity Contracts," *Journal of Financial Economics*, 3 (March 1976), 167–79.

$$d_2 = \frac{\log(F/K) - \frac{\sigma^2}{2}(T^* - t)}{\sigma\sqrt{T^* - t}}$$

COMPUTER TUTORIAL

Computing options values for options on foreign currencies is exactly the same as computing values for options on stocks except we select Currency under the "Underlying Type" menu. Here is a detailed account of the procedure.

1. Basic setup
   a. Set "Option Type" to Vanilla Call or Vanilla Put.
   b. Set "Evaluation Method" to Analytic.
   c. Set "Underlying Type" to Futures Contract.
2. Set parameters
   a. Set Spot Rate slider display to desired stock price.
   b. Set Strike Price slider display to desired strike price.
   c. Set Interest Rate slider display to desired risk-free rate.
   d. Set Volatility slider display to desired volatility.
   e. Set Div'd Yield slider display to desired dividend yield.
   f. Set Expiry slider display to desired expiry.
3. Options
   a. *Changing expiry units.* To change the expiry units to a different unit of time (e.g., days instead of years), pull down the "Configuration" menu and the submenu Expiry (Units), and select a new set of units.
   b. *Changing the maximum slider value.* Sliders have maximum values so that their values slide smoothly. To change the maximum of a slider, pull down the "Configuration" menu:
      i. To change Stock or Strike, use the Stock submenu (the two have the same maximum).
      ii. To change Interest Rate or Dividend max, use the Risk-Free Rate submenu.
      iii. To change Volatility max, use the Volatility submenu.
   c. *Changing the days in a year.* You may change the number of days used in days-in-a-year computation to 365 (default), 250, or 360. To do this, pull down the "Configuration" menu, and use the Days in Year submenu.

REVIEW QUESTIONS

In the following questions, unless otherwise stated, we will use the following notation:

S = underlying asset price
F = futures price
K = strike price
σ = volatility of S per annum

r = risk-free rate of interest per annum
T = futures delivery date
T^* = options expiration

1. What happens to the value of a futures call option as the expiration date of the option is moved further away from the delivery date? Does the option become more or less valuable? Is the same true for a put option?

Hint: Examining the equation for the futures option price, we see it does depend directly on the futures delivery date. The question then is, does it depend on the delivery date at all? The answer is yes, because the futures value depends on the delivery date. Now what is the answer to question 1?

2. Suppose F is a futures contract with delivery date T on a stock S. Let $C(S)$ be a vanilla European option on F, and let $C(F)$ be a vanilla European option on F. Assume that the expiration date of both options is equal to the delivery date of the futures contract; that is, assume the expiration date is equal to T^*. Does the equality $C(F) = C(S)$ hold? Why? (If you are not sure, use the computer to make some computations.)

3. Suppose now that the option expiration is before the futures delivery date.

    a. Is there any set relationship between the value of the futures option and the cash option? For example, is $C(F)$ always less valuable than $C(S)$?

    b. Is there any set relationship between the value of the futures option and the cash option? For example, is $P(F)$ always less valuable than $P(S)$?

4. Do you think put-call parity holds for options on futures? If so, what do you think the formula is? Verify your guess with some numerical examples (see below for suggested numerics, if you wish). (Hint: Look at the formula for an option on a futures contract. It does not depend on what the risk-free interest rate is.)

In the questions that follow, let

$$S = 100$$
$$F = 105$$
$$K = 100$$
$$\sigma = 15\%$$
$$t = \text{today}$$
$$T = 6 \text{ months from today}$$
$$T^* = 4 \text{ months from today}$$

5. Compute the value of $C(F, K, T^*)$ (i.e., the value of a European call on F, struck at). Compute the value of $P(F, K, T)$. What is $C(F, K, T^*) - P(F, K, T)$?

6. Let F be a futures contract on the Standard & Poor's 500 with a time to maturity of three months. Suppose the S&P 500 is trading at 624.54, the futures contract is trading at 634, and the S&P 500 volatility is at 15%. What is the value of a European call expiring in three months on the futures contract? What is the value of an option on the underlying? Explain the difference in value.

7. The theoretical value of an option on a futures contract does not depend on the risk-free rate of interest (according to Black's model). The theoretical values of options on the underlying do. Does this make valuing an option on a futures contract a safer bet than valuing the same option on the underlying?

Solutions

Problem 2

To answer this question, let's first do an experiment: Set time to expiry on the options calculator to 1 year, set the futures price to 100 and the strike to 100. Also set the risk-free rate to 10 percent and the volatility to 15 percent. The option on the future under these conditions has a Black's formula value of $5.41. Let's assume the future is trading at the theoretically correct price for a forward contract. Then the stock price must be

$$S = e^{-rT}F,$$

or $S = e^{-0.10}100 = 90.48$. Now we find the Black-Scholes value of the European call on the stock with this price. Indeed the answer is the same: $5.41.

This answer is intuitively correct. The two contracts have economically equivalent deliverables: The option on the stock delivers the right to buy the stock, while the option on the future delivers the right to buy the future. But the future is being delivered on its delivery date, and therefore converts immediately to the stock.

6

HEDGE PARAMETERS FOR EUROPEAN OPTIONS AND THE BLACK-SCHOLES FORMULA

REVIEW OF CONCEPTS

Hedge parameters measure the sensitivity of an option price to its various input parameters. Let

S = stock price
K = strike price
σ = volatility per annum
r = risk-free rate of interest per annum
q = dividend yield per annum
$T - t$ = time to expiration

The formulas for the hedge parameters for European call options are as follows:

Symbol	Name	Formula
Δ	Delta	$e^{-q(T-t)}N(d_1)$
Γ	Gamma	$\dfrac{N'(d_1)e^{-q(T-t)}}{S\sigma\sqrt{T-t}}$
ν	Vega	$S\sqrt{T-t}\cdot N'(d_1)e^{-q(T-t)}$
Θ	Theta	$-\dfrac{SN'(d_1)\sigma e^{-q(T-t)}}{2\sqrt{T-t}} - rKe^{-r(T-t)}N(d_2) + qSN(d_1)e^{-q(T-t)}$
ρ	Rho	$K(T-t)e^{-r(T-t)}N(d_2)$

The formulas for the hedge parameters for European put options are as follows:

Symbol	Name	Formula
Δ	Delta	$e^{-q(T-t)}(N(d_1) - 1)$
Γ	Gamma	$\dfrac{N'(d_1)e^{-q(T-t)}}{S\sigma\sqrt{T-t}}$
ν	Vega	$S\sqrt{T-t} \cdot N'(d_1)e^{-q(T-t)}$
Θ	Theta	$-\dfrac{SN'(d_1)\sigma e^{-q(T-t)}}{2\sqrt{T-t}} + rKe^{-r(T-t)}N(-d_2) - qSN(-d_1)e^{-q(T-t)}$
ρ	Rho	$-K(T-t)e^{-r(T-t)}N(-d_2)$

where

$$d_1 = \frac{\log(S/K) + (r - q + \sigma^2/2)(T - t)}{\sigma\sqrt{T - t}}$$

$$d_2 = d_1 - \sigma\sqrt{T - t}$$

These formulas are based on the same assumptions as the Black-Scholes formula.

In general, a hedge parameter yields a formula for the approximate value of an option after a small change in an input variable. For example, if S is the current stock price, and δS represents a small change in S, then

$$C(S + \delta S) \approx C(S) + \Delta(\delta S),$$

where $C(S + \delta S)$ represents the value of an option at stock price $S + \delta S$, $C(S)$ represents the value of the same option when the stock price is S, and Δ represents the delta of the option.

Delta Hedging

Delta hedging is a simple trading strategy for hedging the risk of an option. The strategy is that the holder of a short option position should hold Δ shares of the stock at all times. To implement the strategy requires continuous portfolio rebalancing and many assumptions about market mechanics such as infinite liquidity and unrestricted short selling.

COMPUTER TUTORIAL

Computing European call and put option hedge parameters is as easy as clicking the EVALUATE OPTION button. When the Options Calculator evaluates an option it always evaluates the relevant hedge parameters for the option as well. You may compute hedge parameter values for any of the option evaluation methods listed in the "Evaluation Method" menu. The option hedge parameter values are displayed in the two boxes labeled "Greeks: European" and "Greeks: American." Here is a detailed description of what to do:

1. Basic setup
   a. Set "Option Type" to Vanilla Call or Vanilla Put.
   b. Set "Evaluation Method" to Analytic.
   c. Set "Underlying Type" to Stock or Index.

2. Set parameters
   a. Set Stock Price slider display to desired stock price.
   b. Set Strike Price slider display to desired strike price.
   c. Set Interest Rate slider display to desired risk-free rate.
   d. Set Volatility slider display to desired volatility.
   e. Set Div'd Yield slider display to desired dividend yield.
   f. Set Expiry slider display to desired expiry.

3. **Options.** There are many choices available for configuring the finer points of the Options Calculator:
   a. *Changing expiry units.* To change the expiry units to a different unit of time (e.g., days instead of years), pull down the "Configuration" menu and the submenu Expiry (Units), and select a new set of units.
   b. *Changing the expiry units and theta.* The hedge parameter theta is always expressed in the current units of expiry. For example, if the current units of expiry are Years, then the value displayed for theta will mean rate of change of option value per one-year change in time. To see the value of theta in a different set of units, simply pull down the Expiry Units submenu of the "Configuration" menu, and change the units. This will automatically recalculate theta in the new set of units.
   c. *Changing the output precision.* You have a choice between output precision of two or four digits. To change the precision, pull down the "Configuration" menu and the submenu Output Precision. Choose between two and four digits.
   d. *Changing the maximum slider value.* Sliders have maximum values so that their values slide smoothly. To change the maximum of a slider, pull down the "Configuration" menu:
      i. To change *Stock* or *Strike,* use the Stock submenu (the two have the same maximum).
      ii. To change *Interest Rate* or *Dividend* max, use the Risk-Free Rate submenu.
      iii. To change *Volatility* max, use the Volatility submenu.
   e. *Changing the days in a year.* You may change the number of days used in days-in-a-year computation to 365 (default), 250, or 360. To do this, pull down the "Configuration" menu and use Days in Year submenu.

4. *Pricing an option and computing hedge parameters.* Once all parameters have been selected, click the EVALUATE OPTION pushbutton. The price of the option will be displayed in the European Value display box.

Graphing Hedge Parameter Values

You may make two- and three-dimensional graphs of option hedge parameter values. Making graphs proceeds exactly the same as in producing graphs of option values. You may plot any of the hedge parameters—delta, gamma, theta, vega, or rho—versus any of the input parameters. The procedure works exactly the same as for plotting Black-Scholes option prices.

There is one additional plotting option that pertains especially to hedge parameters. The Delta Portfolio allows you to plot the value of a delta neutral portfolio. Here is how it works:

- Set the "Plot Z" pulldown menu to Delta Portfolio.
- Set the "X-Axis" pulldown menu to whatever values you wish.
- Set the input parameters to whatever values you wish.
- Press the PLOT X-Z button.

After depressing the PLOT X-Z button, the Options Calculator proceeds in the following steps:

- It computes the value Δ of the option delta for the current set of input parameters. That is, the Calculator reads the slider displays, collects all the input parameters, and computes Δ.
- The options calculator then makes a graph of

$$\text{Option value} - \Delta \cdot \text{Stock value}$$

allowing whatever parameter is selected in the X-axis to vary as it calculates the option value.

Example Suppose the "Z-Axis" pulldown menu is set to Delta Portfolio, the "X-axis" is set to Stock Price, and the "Option Type" is set to Vanilla Call. Moreover, suppose the input parameters are selected as follows:

$$S = 100$$
$$K = 100$$
$$\sigma = 15\%$$
$$r = 5\%$$
$$q = 0\%$$
$$T = 1 \text{ year}$$

Then

1. The Options Calculator will compute the Black-Scholes delta of a European call with the preceding input parameters.
2. The Options Calculator will graph stock price S versus $C - \Delta S$ as stock price ranges over the values 40 to 140.

QUESTIONS FOR BASIC UNDERSTANDING

Delta

1. The delta of an option is the rate of change of option value to stock price. Set:

$S = 100$
$K = 100$
$\sigma = 15\%$
$r = 5\%$
$q = 0\%$
$T = 1$ year

a. Compute the value of a vanilla European call with these input values, and compute its delta.

b. The delta in the last question is equal to 0.62. This means that for every $1.00 change in stock price, the option value should change approximately $0.62. Verify this statement in four ways:

- Change the price of S to $101. Recompute the call option value and note its change.
- Change the price of S to $100.50. Recompute the call option value. Since the delta is 0.62, the option value should change by approximately $0.31 from its value when the stock price is $100. Why? Does this approximation hold up?
- Change the price of S to $100.25. By approximately how much should the option value change from its value when the stock price is $100? Recompute the call option value. Does this approximation hold up?
- Change the price of S to $99.875. By approximately how much should the option value change from its value when the stock price is $100? Recompute the call option value. Does this approximation hold up?

c. Repeat these exercises for the hedge parameters gamma, theta, vega, and rho.

Delta neutral positions

2. A portfolio is called *delta neutral* if the rate of change of its theoretical value with respect to stock price is zero. Set the input parameter values as follows:

$S = 100$
$K = 100$
$\sigma = 15\%$
$r = 5\%$
$q = 0\%$
$T = 1$ year

We know from our basic study of options pricing that

$$C - \Delta S$$

is delta neutral. That is, the position consisting of delta shares of the stock short and one option long is delta neutral. This exercise will study the meaning of the delta neutrality of this portfolio. Complete the following exercises.

     a. Make a graph of stock price S versus $C - \Delta S$ using the Options Calculator. What is the shape of the graph?

     b. What is the financial meaning of the shape of this graph?

     c. What is the mathematical explanation for the shape of this graph?

     d. What is the significance of this for hedging a short option position?

Discussion

The graph of stock price versus portfolio value is parabolic in shape. That is, it has the basic shape of the graph $y = x^2$. Financially, the graph has a single minimum point, located at the current value of S. All other values in the graph are greater than this value. Financially speaking this means that the portfolio's value is the least at the current stock price and will increase if the current stock price moves.

The mathematical explanation for this phenomenon has two origins: the Taylor series expansion of option value in stock price and the gamma of the option. The theorem on Taylor series[1] states that

$$C(S + \delta S) = C(S) + \Delta(\delta S) + \frac{1}{2}\Gamma(\delta S)^2 + \text{Small error} \qquad (2)$$

where

$$
\begin{aligned}
S &= \text{stock price} \\
\delta S &= \text{a small change in stock price} \\
C(S) &= \text{value of option when stock price is } S \\
\Delta &= \text{delta of option when stock price is } S \\
\Gamma &= \text{gamma of option when stock price is } S
\end{aligned}
$$

We will not discuss the details of the small error here.

If we substitute the expression in equation (2) into the expression $C(S + \delta S) - \Delta(S + \delta S)$ we obtain

$$C(S + \delta S) - \Delta(S + \delta S) = C(S) + \Delta(\delta S) + \frac{1}{2}\Gamma(\delta S)^2 - \Delta S - \Delta(\delta S)$$

$$= C(S) - \Delta S + \frac{1}{2}\Gamma(\delta S)^2$$

That is, the portfolio value, up to a small error, changes according to one-half Γ times the square of the change in the stock value. Put another way, for every δS change in stock value, the portfolio will change approximately $(\delta S)^2$ times one-half Γ.

These results have an important impact on the hedging of an option. Suppose we are delta hedging a short option position (see *Black-Scholes and Beyond,* Chapter 5, for a discussion of

---

[1] See any book on elementary calculus for a discussion of the Taylor series.

delta hedging); our position at any given time is then $\Delta S - C$. That is, we are *long* the stock and *short* the option. As a consequence, any change in the stock price will decrease the hedging portfolio value by an amount proportional to Γ times the square of the change in the stock price. As a consequence, the larger Γ is, the more quickly our delta hedged position loses money.

3. Consider the following strategy. Buy a long position in an option on S and short ΔS shares of the stock. From the graph of stock price versus $C - \Delta S$, it seems that as long as stock price moves, we will profit. Is this a foolproof way to make money with options? To help understand this, complete the following exercises:

    a. Set the input parameters to

$$S = 100$$
$$K = 100$$
$$\sigma = 15\%$$
$$r = 5\%$$
$$q = 0\%$$
$$T = 30 \text{ days}$$

    b. Compute the value of the portfolio $C - \Delta S$ using the Options Calculator.

    c. Now set the input parameters to

$$S = 98$$
$$K = 100$$
$$\sigma = 15\%$$
$$r = 5\%$$
$$q = 0\%$$
$$T = 10 \text{ days}$$

That is, assume that over 20 days the stock price dropped $1.00. Recompute the value of the portfolio.

    d. Now set $S = 102$ with all of the other parameters remaining the same. Recompute the value of the portfolio.

    e. What can you conclude about the strategy of buying $C - \Delta S$ and holding?

Discussion

The strategy of buying the option and shorting the stock does not work because of theta. As time passes, the option's value naturally decreases, lowering the value of the portfolio $C - \Delta S$.

REVIEW QUESTIONS

For the first set of questions, set the input parameters as follows unless otherwise instructed:

$$S = 100$$
$$K = 100$$
$$\sigma = 15\%$$
$$r = 5\%$$
$$T = 1 \text{ year}$$
$$q = 0$$

1. Compute $C(S, K, \sigma, r, T, q)$, and record the value for future reference. Now set $S_1 = 100.5$ and compute $C(S_1, K, \sigma, r, T, q)$. Now compute

$$\frac{C(S_1, K, \sigma, r, T, q) - C(S, K, \sigma, r, T, q)}{0.5}$$

Compute $\Delta(S, K, \sigma, r, T, q)$ using the option calculator; that is, compute the Black-Scholes value of the delta of the option when $S = 100$, $K = 100$, etc. Compare the value of the delta with the previous value. Why are they similar?

2. Now set $S_2 = 100.25$, and recompute the option value and

$$\frac{C(S_2, K, \sigma, r, T, q) - C(S, K, \sigma, r, T, q)}{0.25}$$

If you made your computations correctly, your new value should be closer to the delta. Why? Repeat the exercise with $S_3 = 100.125$; that is, compute

$$\frac{C(S_3, K, \sigma, r, T, q) - C(S, K, \sigma, r, T, q)}{0.125}$$

For the next several exercises we will hedge parameters to predict option prices.

3. Recall the value of $C(S, K, \sigma, r, T, q)$, and compute the Black-Scholes vega of the option. Now set $\sigma_1 = 16\%$, and, using the vega, "predict" the value of $C(S, K, \sigma_1, \sigma, r, T, q)$. Hint: Use the formula (see formula (4.10.1), *Black-Scholes and Beyond*, p. 163)

$$C(\sigma + \Delta\sigma) \simeq C(\sigma) + \nu\Delta\sigma$$

where ν represents the vega of the option and $\Delta\sigma$ represents a change in σ.] Check your answer using the computer.

4. Compute the theta of the option $\Theta(S, K, \sigma, r, T, q)$. Now set T_1 equal to 51 weeks (one year less a week), and, using the same method as given earlier, "predict" the value $C(S, K, \sigma, r, T_1, q)$.

5. For the values of the input parameters given earlier, answer the following question. If the risk-free rate of interest changes 1 percent, how much, approximately, will the option value change? Use hedge parameters to estimate your answer, and then obtain the exact answer by computing the Black-Scholes value of the option with the new risk-free rate.

6. Repeat question 5, but now assume that risk-free rates change by 0.5 percent.

7. Repeat questions 5 and 6, replacing interest rates with volatility.

Option Sensitivities 2

The next set of questions will help improve your understanding of options sensitivities. In all cases, when we refer to an option we mean a vanilla European option. You should use the values of various hedge parameters to obtain your answers. All of the problems require you to "experiment" with the numbers. Try a variety of computations to help determine the solution. Unless otherwise stated, answer the questions for vanilla European put and call options. Suggested method of attack:

- For a given question, first think about the answer intuitively. Review the relevant section in *Black-Scholes and Beyond* to familiarize yourself with the material.
- If you have an intuitive idea of what the answer should be, confirm the answer by making some computations with the computer.
- If you have no idea what the answer should be, make some sample computations to guide yourself.

To help show you what we mean by this method of attack, we have provided a sample solution to question 8.

8. Given an option with one year to maturity, for what *moneyness* is the option most sensitive to changes in the underlying's price: in-the-money, out-of-the-money, or at-the-money?

Sample Solution

Intuitively, we know that deep in-the-money options behave much like the underlying; that is, a dollar change in the value of the underlying results in a dollar change in the value of the option. Moreover, we know that sensitivity to price of the underlying is measured by the delta, and delta is greatest near one. Thus, we guess that the option is most sensitive to the value of the underlying when the option is deep in-the-money. First we set $K = 100$, $\sigma = 15\%$, $r = 5\%$, and $T = 1$ year to expiration, and compute the value of a European call option for $S = 90, 100, 110$, and 120. We find:

$$C(90) = 0.3844 \quad C(100) = 0.6585 \quad C(110) = 0.8517 \quad C(120) = 0.9478$$

which indicates that, as the option moves from out-of-the-money to in-the-money, the delta rises, and hence the option becomes more sensitive to changes in the underlying.

We repeat these computations, this time with time at one week ($T = 1/52$). We obtain

$$C(90) = 0.0000002796 \quad C(100) = 0.5226 \quad C(110) = 0.999998 \quad C(120) = 1.000000$$

9. Does increasing the dividend rate of the underlying make the option more or less sensitive to changes in the price of the underlying? Explain intuitively.

10. For what moneyness is the delta of a vanilla European call close to 1? Close to zero? For what moneyness is the delta of a vanilla European put close to -1? Close to zero?

11. Let C be a European call option and P be a European put on the same underlying with the same strike and same time to expiration. Verify for a few computations the identity:

$$\Delta_P = \Delta_C - 1$$

12. Set $K = 100$, $r = 5\%$, $q = 0$, $\sigma = 10\%$, and $T = 1$ month. For what value of S is $C(S, K, \sigma, r, T, q)$ equal to 0.50? (Hint: Use a method similar to the method of bisections to pinpoint your answer. See *Black-Scholes and Beyond,* pp. 330–36.)

13. In general, does decreasing the time to expiration increase or decrease an option's sensitivity to changes in the underlying's price?

14. In general, does increasing the risk-free rate of interest increase or decrease an option's sensitivity to changes in the underlying's price?

15. In general, does increasing the volatility of the underlying increase or decrease an option's sensitivity to changes in the underlying's price?

16. For a given time to expiration and moneyness (i.e., in-the-, out-of-the-, or at-the-money), does increasing risk-free rates increase or decrease an option's sensitivity to changes in the volatility of the underlying?

17. Suppose we start with an option one year to expiration that is at-the-money. If it remains at-the-money for its entire tenor, does its gamma increase or decrease? (Hint: Try a graph.)

18. Guess intuitively when a European put option might have a positive theta. Put another way, in what situation might a European put option become more valuable as time to expiration decreases? Verify this by making some computations using the computer.

19. Do you think there is any limit to how large the gamma of a vanilla call or put option can become? (Hint: Compute the gamma of at-the-money options near to expiration.)

20. For what moneyness is the theta of an option most negative; that is, for what moneyness is time decay greatest?

21. As time to expiration nears, does the theta of a given option increase or decrease if all other input parameters do not change? Answer the question first for calls and then for puts.

22. If volatility of the underlying increases, does the theta of a call and/or a put increase or decrease?

Delta Hedging

23. This exercise will take you through the process of tabulating the hedging costs in a simple delta hedging strategy. Set the input parameters as follows:

$$S = 100$$
$$K = 100$$
$$\sigma = 15\%$$
$$r = 5\%$$
$$q = 0\%$$
$$T = 10 \text{ days}$$

Table 1 is a price series for 10 days of stock price movements. You are short an option on the stock described by the preceding data and are delta hedging it. Fill in the table using the Options Calculator to make the computations. The following is a brief description of each column of Table 1:

- **Days to expiry.** You are entering into the option position with 10 days to expiry. When you compute the delta of the option, this is the time to expiry to use.
- **Stock price (S).** This is the price of the underlying stock at the time you rebalance.
- **Option delta (Δ).** This is the value of the option at the time you rebalance. With 10 days to expiry, the option has a delta of 0.53.
- **ΔS.** This is the value of the delta-hedged position you are holding. With 10 days to expiry, this position is worth $53.
- **Rebalancing costs.** You have to readjust your position each time according to how the delta changed over the previous day. For example, from the 11th day to 10th

TABLE 1

Price Time Series for the Underlying Stock of an Option with 10 Days to Expiry

Fill in the table with the value of Δ, ΔS (the delta times the stock price), and the rebalancing costs.

Days to Expiry	S	Δ	ΔS	Rebalancing Costs	Total Cost to Date
11	$101.00	0.68	$68.08	N/A	$0.00
10	$100.00	0.53	$53.00	−$15.00	−$15.00
9	100.50				
8	99.875				
7	100.00				
6	100.25				
5	100.50				
4	100.75				
3	100.50				
2	100.50				
1	100.25				
0	100.50				

day the delta dropped from 0.68 to 0.53. Thus, rebalancing took 0.15 share off of the hedge and raised $15 in cash.

- **Total cost to date.** You have to compute the total cost to date of the hedging procedure each time. This amounts to adding the amount of money raised from the sale of stock or subtracting the amount of money spent buying stock to the total after each rebalancing.

Now answer the following questions concerning the delta hedging experiment:

a. At expiration (time zero), what was the delta of the option?

b. How much does the short option position pay the long option position at expiration?

c. What was the option premium with 11 days to expiration?

d. Now imagine you sold the option to a client with 11 days to expiration. At that point you were long the option. How much would you have to have sold the option to the client for in order to break-even?

e. What is the implied volatility of the option at the break-even price of the option?

Solutions

Problems 1 and 2

We start by carrying out the computation in detail for question 1.

$$C(S, K, \sigma, r, T, q) = \$11.51$$

$$C(S_1, K, \sigma, r, T, q) = \$11.94$$

Now, we have

$$\frac{C(S_1, K, \sigma, r, T, q) - C(S, K, \sigma, r, T, q)}{.5} = \frac{11.94 - 11.51}{.25} = 0.86$$

On the other hand, looking at the Options Calculator Greeks display we see that the delta is equal to 0.78.

We now repeat the calculation using S_2 instead of S_1:

$$C(S, K, \sigma, r, T, q) = \$11.51$$

$$C(S_2, K, \sigma, r, T, q) = \$11.72$$

Now, we have

$$\frac{C(S_2, K, \sigma, r, T, q) - C(S, K, \sigma, r, T, q)}{.5} = \frac{11.72 - 11.51}{.25} = 0.84$$

We now repeat the calculation using S_3 instead of S_2:

$$C(S, K, \sigma, r, T, q) = \$11.51$$

$$C(S_3, K, \sigma, r, T, q) = \$11.61$$

Now, we have

$$\frac{C(S_3, K, \sigma, r, T, q) - C(S, K, \sigma, r, T, q)}{.5} = \frac{11.61 - 11.51}{.25} = 0.80$$

Discussion: In each successive computation the value of S_* (S_1, S_2, and S_3) became closer to the value of S. As such, the approximation to the value of Δ became closer as well.

Additional computations: Now choose stock prices S_4, S_5, S_6, etc. such that each successive stock price is closer to $100 than the previous. Recompute the formula

$$\frac{C(S_2, K, \sigma, r, T, q) - C(S, K, \sigma, r, T, q)}{S_i - S}$$

for each number and observe the "convergence" to the delta.

7

⑥ OPTIONS ON CURRENCIES USING THE BLACK-SCHOLES FORMULA

REVIEW OF CONCEPTS

The material in the section was not covered in *Black-Scholes and Beyond* but is fundamentally similar to the ideas there, so we briefly cover it.

BASIC ASSUMPTIONS

Let S be the spot exchange rate. This is the value of one unit of the foreign currency in U.S. dollars. We assume that S follows a geometric Brownian motion with volatility σ; moreover, we assume that the risk-free rate of interest is r. Because there are two currencies in this picture, we refer to r as the domestic risk-free rate. In addition, to value options on a currency (i.e., options on S), we need to assume that there is a foreign risk-free rate of interest. We denote this r_f. Finally, we let K be the strike price of the option (the spot exchange rate you may buy or sell the foreign currency at if you exercise the call or put).

The notation may be summarized as follows:

S = spot exchange rate
K = strike exchange rate
r = domestic risk-free rate
r_f = foreign risk-free rate
σ = volatility of spot exchange rate

Let C be a vanilla European call option on S with the preceding input data. Let P be a vanilla European put option on S with the preceding input data. Then the Black-Scholes formula for C and P are given by

$$C = N(d_1)Se^{-r_f(T-t)} - e^{-r(T-t)}N(d_2)K$$

$$P = -N(-d_1)Se^{-r_f(T-t)} + e^{-r(T-t)}N(-d_2)K$$

where

$$d_1 = \frac{\log(S/K) + (r - r_f + \sigma^2/2)(T - t)}{\sigma\sqrt{T - t}}$$

$$d_2 = d_1 - \sigma\sqrt{T - t}$$

COMPUTER TUTORIAL

Computing options values for options on foreign currencies is exactly the same as computing values for options on stocks except we select Currency under the "Underlying Type" menu. Here is a detailed account of the procedure:

1. Basic setup
   a. Set "Option Type" to Vanilla Call or Vanilla Put.
   b. Set "Evaluation Method" to Analytic.
   c. Set "Underlying Type" to Currency.
2. Set parameters
   a. Set Spot Rate slider display to desired stock price.
   b. Set Strike Price slider display to desired strike price.
   c. Set Interest Rate slider display to desired risk-free rate.
   d. Set Volatility slider display to desired volatility.
   e. Set Foreign Interest Rate slider display to desired level of foreign interest rate.
   f. Set Expiry slider display to desired expiry.
   g. Options
      i. *Changing expiry units.* To change the expiry units to a different unit of time (e.g., days instead of years), pull down the "Configuration" menu and the submenu Expiry (Units), and select a new set of units.
      ii. *Changing the maximum slider value.* Sliders have maximum values so that their values slide smoothly. To change the maximum of a slider, pull down the "Configuration" menu:

      • To change Stock or Strike, use the Stock submenu (the two have the same maximum).
      • To change Interest Rate or Dividend max, use the Risk-Free Rate submenu.
      • To change Volatility max, use the Volatility submenu.

      iii. *Changing the days in a year.* You may change the number of days used in days-in-a-year computation to 365 (default), 250, or 360. To do this, pull down the "Configuration" menu and use the Days in Year submenu.
3. Price the option. Once all parameters have been selected, click the EVALUATE OPTION pushbutton. The price of the option will be displayed in European Value display box.

Graphing Option Values

To graph the value of an option proceed as follows:

1. Choose the type of option to evaluate from the "Option Type" menu.
2. Choose the method of evaluation from the "Evaluation Method" menu.
3. Choose the type of underlying from the "Underlying Type" menu.
   a. Choose a value for the X-axis. Pull down the X-axis menu and choose the value to vary for the X-axis.
   b. Choose a value for the Z-axis. Pull down the Z-axis menu and choose a value for the Z-axis (vertical axis) of the graph. To plot option value choose Plot Option.
   c. Plot the option. Press PLOT X-Z.

REVIEW QUESTIONS

1. Holding a foreign currency is analogous to holding a stock with a continuous dividend yield (see, e.g., *Black-Scholes and Beyond,* pp. 48–53). Use this fact and an arbitrage argument to derive the Black-Scholes formula for options on foreign currencies. (Hint: see *Black-Scholes and Beyond* p. 159.)

2. Suppose we are long an option on Deutschmarks with a strike exchange rate of K (with current dollar/mark spot rate equal to S). This position can be expressed by saying that we have an option to buy K units of Deutschmark for $1. Express this as a position in an option to buy or sell dollars with Deutschmarks.

3. Find a put-call parity relationship for European currency options. (Hint: Use the value of a forward position in a foreign currency, and imitate the derivation of put-call parity for ordinary options.)

8

⊚ BLACK-SCHOLES IMPLIED VOLATILITY

REVIEW OF CONCEPTS

Implied volatility is the concept of the correct volatility that *implies* a given option price. It is used to derive a "market" estimate of volatility on the underlying asset of a traded option. If an option is traded, its price is set by some mechanism. We can back out from this the volatility one would have to use in the Black-Scholes formula to produce this price.

The key issues concerning implied volatility are how one computes it. There are two methods discussed in *Black-Scholes and Beyond:*

- The Newton-Raphson method.
- The method of bisections.

The Newton-Raphson Method

The Newton-Raphson method relies on knowing the vega of the option (see Chapter 6). Consider the following scenario. We have a call option C on a stock S. We have the following information:

S = stock price
K = strike price
r = risk-free rate
q = dividend yield
T = time to expiry
C = price of the call option

From this information we want to deduce the volatility σ that would make the Black-Scholes price of an option with input parameters S, K, r, and T, equal to C.

The Newton-Raphson method then proceeds in the following manner:

1. Start with an initial volatility guess σ_1.
2. Compute $C(\sigma_1)$, which is the Black-Scholes value of an option with input parameters S, K, r, T, and σ_1.
3. Compute $V(\sigma_1)$, which is the Black-Scholes vega of an option with input parameters S, K, r, T, and σ_1.
4. Compute

$$\sigma_2 = \sigma_1 - \frac{C(\sigma_1) - C}{V(\sigma_1)}$$

5. Repeat steps 1, 2, 3, and 4 by replacing σ_1 with σ_2.
6. Continue by producing the n'th volatility guess from the $n - 1$st by computing

$$\sigma_n = \sigma_{n-1} - \frac{C(\sigma_{n-1}) - C}{V(\sigma_{n-1})}$$

7. Stop the process when the value of $C(\sigma_k)$ is satisfactorily close to C.

COMPUTER TUTORIAL

Computing implied volatility using the *Black-Scholes and Beyond Interactive Toolkit* is easy. You may choose between computing with the Newton-Raphson method or the method of bisections. Here is the procedure for computing implied volatility:

1. Basic setup
    a. Set "Option Type" to Vanilla Call or Vanilla Put. This will determine the type of option for which Black-Scholes implied volatility is produced.
    b. Set "Evaluation Method" to Analytic.
    c. Set "Underlying Type" to Stock or Index.
2. Set parameters
    a. Set Stock Price slider display to desired stock price.
    b. Set Strike Price slider display to desired strike price.
    c. Set Interest Rate slider display to desired risk-free rate.
    d. Set Div'd Yield slider display to desired dividend yield.
    e. Set Expiry slider display to desired expiry.
    f. Keep in mind that you do not need to set the volatility slider. In fact, it does not matter what value is in the volatility box prior to computing implied volatility. Whatever value is there will be replaced by the implied volatility of the option you compute.
    g. Options:
        i. *Choosing the method of computation.* The Options Calculator can be set to compute implied volatility using either the Newton-Raphson method or the method of bisections. To set the method, pull down the "Implied Volatility" menu, and select the menu corresponding to the method of your choice.

ii. *Changing expiry units.* To change the expiry units to a different unit of time (e.g., days instead of years), pull down the "Configuration" menu and the submenu Expiry (Units), and select a new set of units.

iii. *Changing the output precision.* You have a choice between output precision of two or four digits. To change the precision, pull down the "Configuration" menu and the submenu Output Precision. Choose between two and four digits.

iv. *Changing the maximum slider value.* Sliders have maximum values so that their values slide smoothly. To change the maximum of a slider, pull down the "Configuration" menu:

- To change Stock or Strike, use the Stock submenu (the two have the same maximum).
- To change Interest Rate or Dividend max, use the risk-free rate submenu.
- To change Volatility max, use the Volatility submenu.

v. *Changing the days in a year.* You may change the number of days used in days-in-a-year computation to 365 (default), 250, or 360. To do this, pull down the "Configuration" menu and use the Days in Year submenu.

3. Compute implied volatility. Once all parameters have been selected, click the IMPLIED VOLATILITY pushbutton. The Options Calculator will compute the Black-Scholes implied volatility of the option you have specified using the method you have specified.

a. The calculator will display the implied volatility in the volatility slider display box.

b. The calculator will compute the greeks of the option you have specified to the precision you have specified.

c. If the Options Calculator fails to compute the implied volatility, or if there is an input error, an error box will appear.

QUESTIONS FOR BASIC UNDERSTANDING

For the following exercises, set the output precision to four digits.

1. We begin by making an implied volatility computation. This exercise will enhance your understanding of the Newton-Raphson method. Set

$S = 100$
$K = 100$
$T = 30$ days
$r = 10\%$
$q = 0\%$
$C = \$3.23$

where C is a European call option on S struck at K expiring at T.

Start with an initial guess of $\sigma = 50\%$.

a. Compute $C(\sigma_1)$. That is, compute the Black-Scholes value of a call option with $S = 100$, $K = 100$, $T = 30$ days, $r = 10\%$, and volatility $= 50\%$. (Answer: \$6.1103)

b. Compute $V(\sigma_1)$. That is, compute the Black-Scholes vega of a call option with $S = 100$, $K = 100$, $T = 30$ days, $r = 10\%$, and volatility $= 50\%$. (Answer: 0.1134)

    c. Compute

$$\sigma_2 = \sigma_1 - \frac{C(\sigma_1) - C}{V(\sigma_1)}$$

(Answer: 24.60)
    d. Compute $C(\sigma_2)$ and $V(\sigma_2)$. (Answers: \$3.2297 and 0.1131)
    e. Compute

$$\sigma_3 = \sigma_2 - \frac{C(\sigma_2) - C}{V(\sigma_2)}$$

(Answer: 24.6027)
    f. Compute $C(\sigma_3)$. (Answer: 3.2300)

Note that Newton's method already converged after three iterations, to exactly 3.2300. Therefore, within a tolerance of 0.0001, the method has converged, and the Black-Scholes implied volatility is 24.6027%.

    Confirm your answer using the Options Calculator implied volatility feature. Note that the calculator lists the implied volatility as 24.67%. This difference in the fourth decimal place (.2467 versus .2460) is accounted for by the rounding that took place.

    2. Set

$$S = 100$$
$$K = 102$$
$$T = 1 \text{ year}$$
$$r = 10\%$$
$$C = \$12.23$$

where C is a European call option on S struck at K expiring at T.

    a. Compute the Black-Scholes implied volatility of C using the preceding procedure or the Options Calculator.

    b. Use put-call parity to derive the value of a put option with input parameters S, K, T, and r. Write P for this put value (see Chapter 1 of this book).

    c. Compute the Black-Scholes implied volatility of P using the Options Calculator.

    If you did the computations correctly, the implied volatility of P should equal the implied volatility of C. Why is this the case? (Hint: It has to do with the fundamental assumptions of Black-Scholes.)

    Food for thought: Recall that the existence of the volatility smile suggests that volatility of stock price processes may not be constant. Does this mean that put-call parity can be violated?

    3. Set

$$S = 100$$
$$K = 100$$
$$T = 1 \text{ year}$$
$$r = 10\%$$
$$\sigma = 30\%$$

These are exactly the same parameters as given earlier except that $K = 100$ instead of $K = 102$. Use the Options Calculator to compute the Black-Scholes implied volatility for C.

 a. Make a graph of Black-Scholes European call option value versus volatility (set the X-axis to Volatility and the Z-axis to Option Value).

 b. Choose any point on the vertical axis (e.g., $8) that has a tick mark, and note the option value the tick-mark corresponds to.

 c. Move the mouse pointer horizontally on the screen until it meets the graph, then move the mouse pointer vertically down the screen until it hits the X-axis.

 d. Record the value on the X-axis (e.g., if the number is approximately 32%, remember this).

 e. Now enter the previous number into the volatility slider box in the Options Calculator, leaving all other parameters the same; compute the European call value.

 f. The call value should correspond roughly to the value you marked on the vertical axis. Why?

REVIEW QUESTIONS

The following questions will help build your intuition about implied volatility. Use the Options Calculator to obtain answers to the following questions.

 1. We have the following set of input parameters:

S = stock price
K = strike price
r = risk-free rate
q = dividend yield
T = time to expiry
C = price of the call option

 a. If we raise the risk-free rate of interest and keep all of the other parameters fixed, does implied volatility go up or down?

 b. If we raise the dividend yield and keep all of the other parameters fixed, does implied volatility go up or down?

 c. Is it true that the effect of interest rates on implied volatility is the same regardless of the moneyness of the option?

 2. Earlier we studied the formula for at-the-money forward options:

$$C = \frac{1}{\sqrt{2\pi}}\sigma\sqrt{T}e^{-rT}$$

where

K = strike price
S = stock price
r = risk-free interest rate
T = time to expiry

Answer the following questions:

    a. Use the preceding equation to derive a formula for implied volatility for at-the-money forward options.

    b. Verify that the formula is accurate. Can you determine the degree of accuracy for the formula?

    c. As time to expiry increases, does the formula become more or less accurate?

    d. As volatility increases, does the formula become more or less accurate?

    3. Derive a formula for implied volatility of an at-the-money forward put option, based on the above formula.

    4. Derive a formula for the vega of an at-the-money forward call option, based on the above formulas (the solution of the problem requires the knowledge of differential calculus).

    5. Answer questions 1 and 2 for the approximate formula for the vega of an at-the-money forward option.

Solutions

Problem 1

The point of this question is to see the effect of changing various parameters on the price of an option. To answer, we start by building our intuition by making some computations on the optimus calculator, and then attempt to explain our observations with theory and intuition.

    a. Set $S = 100, K = 100, r = 10$ percent, $q = 0$ percent and T to 30 days, and $C = \$5.00$. Using the options calculator, we find that the implied volatility of C is 40.217 percent. Now, here is a chart of the implied volatility of the same options for various other interest rates:

Interest rate	Implied Volatility
5%	41.997%
6	41.645
7	41.291
8	40.935
9	40.577
10	40.217
11	39.854
12	39.488

    We see that the implied volatilities steadily decrease (albeit slowly) as the risk-free rate increases. What does this imply? To answer this, we have to answer the more basic question: Since the option's price has remained the same, what is the economic meaning of a change in implied volatility? Recall that all things being equal, an increase in volatility entails an increase in option value. On the other hand, we have held the option value at a constant $5.00.

    To resolve this seeming contradiction, recall that the *rho* of a European call option is always positive. Put another way, an increase in interest rate prices entails an increase in option value. Therefore, when we increased the interest rates above, we were necessarily raising the option value. But implied volatility answers the question: What volatility makes the option value equal to a given price? Since raising the interest rate raised the values of the option, it was necessary to lower the volatility to counter this effect.

b. Let's proceed as in *a*, by first making a chart. We will use the same set of input parameters as above, and set $r = 10\%$.

Dividend yield	Option value
0%	40.217%
1	40.613
2	41.007
3	41.399
4	41.789
5	42.117
6	42.5644

We see that increasing the dividend yield *increases* implied volatility. On the other hand, we know that increasing dividend yield decreases option value. Therefore, applying the same logic as in part *a*, we see that if raising an input parameter's value increases option values, then raising the same parameter's value will decrease implied volatility (of a fixed option value). Conversely, if raising an input parameter's value decreases option value, implied volatility will increase.

c. We can answer this question without doing any computations, based on our experience with questions *a* and *b*. We know that the *rho* of a European call option is *always* positive. Thus, raising interest rates will *always* increase the value of a call option, and therefore raising interest rates will always decrease implied volatility.

Problem 2

a. This question gives a formula for at-the-money forward implied options. (Recall: At-the-money forward means the current stock price is equal to the strike price discounted from expiration to today at the risk-free rate, that is, $S = e^{-rT}K$.) We do this by solving for σ directly and obtain:

$$\sigma = \sqrt{2\pi}e^{-rT}C/\sqrt{T}.$$

In the above equation, the left-hand side represents implied volatility, and the value of C in the right-hand side is the value of the input option.

To verity this formula we make a chart with three columns: 1) C, the value of the call option, 2) σ_{approx}, the *approximate* value of implied volatility using the above formula, and 3) σ_{iv}, the value of implied volatility obtained using the Newton-Raphson method. We set the input parameters to

$$S = 99.1815$$
$$K = 100$$
$$r = 10\%$$
$$q = 0\%$$
$$T = 30 \text{ days}$$

In addition, we set the number of days in a year (to set this, pull down the *Configuration menu* to the *Days in year* submenu) to 365. Note also, that the above stock price is exactly equal to the strike price discounted by 30 days at a 10 percent interest rate, that is:

$$99.1815 = e^{-0.10 \cdot 30/365} 100.$$

c	σ_{aprox}	σ_{iv}
$2	17.6309%	17.5188%
2.50	22.0387	22.031
3.50	26.4464	26.440
4.50	39.6696	39.675
5	44.0773	44.090
6	52.8928	52.925

We see that the approximation is very close, accurate to approximately one-tenth of 1 percent.

Now to answer question c, let's make another chart of implied volatilities, but this time with the time to expiry equal to one year, that is, $T = 1$. We therefore also must set $S = 90.4837$ so that the option is still at-the-money forward.

c	σ_{aprox}	σ_{iv}
$10	27.7025%	27.7868%
11	30.4728	30.5870
12	33.2430	33.3930
13	36.0133	36.2063
14	38.7835	39.0265
15	41.5538	41.8536

We see that as the time to expiry increased, the accuracy of the basic formula decreased.

9

⑥ THE CONSTRUCTION OF BINOMIAL TREES

REVIEW OF CONCEPTS

Constructing Binomial Trees

A binomial tree is a stock price model in which time is discrete and where, at any given moment of time (represented by the model), a stock price will either move up by a certain amount or move down by a certain amount over the next time period. The tree consists of stock price nodes. The first node of the tree is called the vertex node, and the final nodes of the tree are called terminal nodes. The following is an example of a binomial tree:

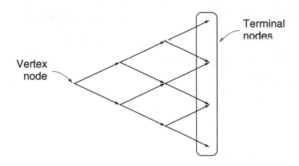

Cox-Ross-Rubinstein trees

Cox-Ross-Rubinstein trees are specified by the following variables:

S = initial stock price
r = risk-free rate of interest per annum
σ = volatility per annum

q = annualized dividend rate
t = start date
T = end date
Δt = length of time step
n = number of periods

Note that the number of periods is defined so that $n \cdot \Delta t = T - t$, where $T - t$ is the time from start to finish.

Later we will show how to add a dividend schedule. Given the preceding data, we set the up-ratio u and the down ratio d to

$$u = e^{\sqrt{\Delta t}\sigma}, \quad d = e^{-\sqrt{\Delta t}\sigma}$$

and the up-transition probability

$$p = \frac{e^{(r-q)\Delta t} - d}{u - d}$$

We refer to the above as the CRR formulas.

Cox-Ross-Rubinstein trees can sometimes produce negative transition probabilities: When interest rate levels are high and volatility levels are low, this can happen. When this happens, the trees cannot be used to price options. In such a case, you have to use a different type of tree, such as equal probability trees.

Equal Probability Trees

Equal probability trees derive their names from the fact that the up and down transition probabilities are always equal to 50%. The main advantage of equal probability trees is that they never, by definition, produce negative probabilities.

Equal probability trees are specified by the following variables:

S = initial stock price
r = risk-free rate of interest per annum
σ = volatility per annum
q = annualized dividend rate
t = start date
T = end date
Δt = length of time step
n = number of periods

The formulas for the up and down ratios are as follows:

$$d = \frac{2e^{\mu \Delta t}}{e^{2\sigma\sqrt{\Delta t}} + 1}$$

$$u = \frac{2e^{\mu \Delta t + 2\sigma\sqrt{\Delta t}}}{e^{2\sigma\sqrt{\Delta t}} + 1}$$

The key concepts are local volatility, transition probability, and Arrow Debreu price. Given an up-transition probability of p and a one-period piece of a binomial tree as such:

The local volatility σ_{loc} at the vertex is given by the formula

$$\sigma_{\text{loc}} = \frac{1}{\Delta t} \sqrt{p(1-p)} \log(S_u/S_d)$$

The Arrow-Debreu price of a node is the "present value" of the probability of arriving at that node. Put another way, it is the value of a financial instrument that pays \$1 if the node is reached and nothing otherwise.

Dividends and Binomial Trees

There are two ways to add dividends to binomial trees. The first, discussed earlier, is to add a discrete time dividend yield as a percentage of spot price at each node of the tree. The other method is to add lumpy dividends into the tree. We do this in the following steps:

1. Produce a dividend schedule for the binomial tree: $(D_0, 0), \ldots, (D_N, N)$, where D_i is the dividend payment for time i of the tree. [1] If t_i is not an ex-dividend date, then D_i is set to zero.

2. Compute the present value of all future dividend payments in the schedule; this means we compute

$$\mathcal{D} = \sum_{i=0}^{N} e^{-ri\Delta t} D_i$$

where r is the risk-free rate, i represents the i'th time step, and Δt is the length of the time-step so that $i\Delta t$ simply represents $t_i - t_0$, the amount of time from t_0 to t_i.

3. Build a risk-neutral binomial tree starting with a spot price of $S_0 - \mathcal{D}$, using σ as the volatility and r as the risk-free rate.[2]

4. Adjust the nodes for dividend payments: For each time step t_i, compute the present value (at time t_i) of all dividend payments occurring after time t_i. That is, compute

$$\mathcal{D}_i = \sum_{j=i+1}^{N} e^{-r(j-i)\Delta t} D_j$$

---

[1] We regard the vertex of the tree as time 0.
[2] Note: It does not matter what method we use to build the tree as long as it is risk-neutral.

where $(j - i)\Delta t$ represents the amount of time from t_i to t_j. Add to each node at time t_i the value $\mathcal{D}_i$.

COMPUTER TUTORIAL

You can use the *Black-Scholes and Beyond Interactive Toolkit* Options Calculator to build and display binomial trees as well as all of the other types of trees associated with a binomial tree.[3] You can also use the Calculator to display terminal stock price and stock return distributions for trees you construct.

Building Trees on the Options Calculator

To build a Cox-Ross-Rubinstein or equal probabilities tree, proceed as follows:

    1. Set the parameters

$$S = \text{stock price}$$
$$r = \text{interest rate}$$
$$\sigma = \text{volatility}$$
$$q = \text{dividend yield}$$
$$T = \text{expiry}$$

by adjusting the appropriate slider. The variable T determines the amount of time the binomial tree represents. You can build trees on any of the following underlying types by setting the "Underlying Type" to the corresponding item:

    a. Stock or Index.
    b. Currency.
    c. Futures Contract.

    2. Adjust the expiry units. Go to the "Configuration" menu, and select the Expiry (Units) submenu, and then select from Days, Weeks, Months, or Years. This will change the units you can enter into the Expiry slider.

You may also enter an option dividend schedule for the construction of the tree. It is important to note that you do not have to enter ex-dividend dates that correspond to the nodes of the tree.

    a. Enter a dividend schedule by proceeding in the following manner:
        i. Create a dividend schedule.

$$(t_1, D_1), (t_2, D_2), \ldots, (t_k, D_k)$$

        ii. Press the ENTER DIV'DS button.
        iii. Enter the number of dividends payments into the box labeled Number of Dates. For example, if there are eight dividends payments in your dividend schedule, enter 8 dividends.

---

[3] Due to screen space limitations, all displays of binomial trees only show the first 10 time periods.

iv. Press OK to enter the dividend schedule. If you do not wish to press OK, you may do one of two things:

- Press QUIT. This will close the screen, and you will return to the main screen and nothing will change with the system.
- Press CLEAR. This will clear all of the dividends from the system.

After you press OK, a new screen will appear with a list of ex-dates and payments. The top row of boxes represents the ex-dates. Enter the ex-dates in the same units as the expiry. Note: Even though the construction of a binomial tree requires the dividend payments to coincide with the tree nodes, you can enter any ex-dividend you like. The Calculator will estimate the correct dividend dates at the node values. The bottom row represents dividend payments. Enter the dividend payments in dollars.

v. When you are done entering your schedule, press ACCEPT to enter the dividends into the system or QUIT to erase the currently entered dividend schedule. If you QUIT, the dividend schedule that was in the system prior to entering your data will remain.

vi. Evaluate options. Once you enter a dividend schedule into the system, all subsequent option evaluations will assume your underlying has this dividend schedule.

vii. To view or change the dividends, a button will appear if there are dividends currently in the system.

b. Select a type of binomial tree by going to the "Evaluation Method" menu and selecting either Binomial: CRR or Binomial: Equal Prob.

c. Build the tree by pressing the EVALUATE OPTION button. This evaluates an option but also builds the tree.

Displaying Trees

You may use the Options Calculator to display any of the following types of trees: stock price tree, local volatility tree, Arrow-Debreu price tree, and transition probability tree. The Option Calculator allows you to specify the degree of precision (number of decimal places) displayed in the output tree. Here is the procedure for displaying a tree:

1. Build a tree using the method outlined earlier.

2. Select a type of tree (e.g., stock price, Arrow-Debreu price, etc.) to display from the menu directly beneath DISPLAY.

3. Press the DISPLAY button.

4. Options: You may select one of three output precisions for the binomial tree display (two-, four-, or six-digit precision). To select a precision, pull down the "Configuration" menu and select from the Output Precision (trees) submenu.

5. Keep in mind that when you press DISPLAY the Options Calculator looks at the "Evaluation Method" menu to see what the current evaluation method is and then displays the last tree built for that method. This way, you can build more than one type of tree, e.g., a CRR tree and then an equal probabilities tree, and still display the first tree.

For example, if you build a Cox-Ross-Rubinstein tree and then an equal probability tree and decide you want to view the stock price tree from the CRR, simply set the evaluation method to Cox-Ross-Rubinstein, set the "Display ..."menu to Stock Tree, and then press DISPLAY.

After a brief pause, the tree you requested will appear. If the tree in the system is greater than 10 time periods, only the first 10 periods will be displayed. At the bottom of the tree, the system displays the time steps and the dividend payments used to construct the tree.

QUESTIONS FOR BASIC UNDERSTANDING

Revisiting *Black-Scholes and Beyond*

1. Use the *Black-Scholes and Beyond Interactive Toolkit* Options Calculator to reproduce the binomial tree in Figure 6.5.1 on page 235 of *Black-Scholes and Beyond* in the following steps:

    a. Set "Option Type" to Vanilla Call or Vanilla Put.

    b. Set "Evaluation Method" to Binomial: CRR.

    c. Set "Underlying Type" to Stock.

    d. Set the number of time periods to 4 using the expiry slider. To set the Expiry Units to months, go to the "Configuration" menu at the top of the screen, and select the Expiry (Units) submenu.

    e. Set the stock price to $100 using the Stock Price slider.

    f. Set the expiry to 4 months. (Why? Because there are four periods, and Δt is equal to one month.)

    g. Set the volatility to 15% using the Volatility slider.

    h. Set the risk-free interest rate to 10% using the Interest Rate slider.

    i. Set the dividend yield to 0% using the Div'd Yield slider.

    j. Press the EVALUATE OPTION button.

    k. Make sure there are no dividends currently in the system by pressing the ENTER DIV'DS button and then pressing the CLEAR button on the screen that pops up.

    l. Press the DISPLAY TREE button.

A tree equal to the tree in Figure 6.5.1 up to two decimal places will appear. The numbers in Figure 6.5.1 were rounded to two decimal places when the book was produced.

2. Repeat the procedure in the previous exercise to produce the equal probabilities tree in Figure 6.5.2 on page 237 of *Black-Scholes and Beyond*. Note: To enter the correct time to expiry it is necessary to multiply $\Delta t = .0167$ by 4 and enter this into the expiry display. Also, don't forget to set the expiry units to years.

3. Repeat this procedure for the trees in Figure 6.10.3 on page 258 of *Black-Scholes and Beyond*. To enter the dividend at time t_2, follow the procedure outlined in the computer tutorial. (Make sure to enter one tree with an ex-dividend date of two years from today and for $1.)

4. Recreate the histograms in Figure 6.12.3 on page 270 of *Black-Scholes and Beyond* using the following steps:

    a. Set "Option Type" to Vanilla Call or Vanilla Put.

    b. Set "Evaluation Method" to Binomial: CRR.

    c. Set "Underlying Type" to Stock.

    d. Set the number of times to 1 year using the Expiry slider.

    e. Set the stock price to \$100 using the Stock Price slider.

    f. Set the volatility at $\sigma = 15\%$ using the volatility slider.

    g. Set the risk-free rate at $r = 10\%$ using the interest rate slider.

    h. Set the number of periods to 5 using the Periods slider.

    i. Press the EVALUATE OPTION button.

    j. Press the DISTRIBUTION button.

Cox-Ross-Rubinstein Trees

The following questions will reinforce the basic way Cox-Ross-Rubinstein trees are built.

    5. Build a five-period CRR tree with the following data (to build the tree, set the values of the parameters as given, select CRR Tree from the "Option Type" menu, and press EVALUATE OPTION):

$$S = 100$$
$$T = 30 \text{ days}$$
$$\sigma = 15\%$$
$$r = 10\%$$

Answer the following questions:

    a. Display the binomial stock price tree, and verify directly that

$$u = e^{\sigma \sqrt{\Delta t}}$$

$$d = 1/u$$

    b. Display the transition probability tree and verify that all of the transition probabilities are 50%. Now verify this directly from the stock price tree and the formula for transition probability.

    c. Compute the local volatility of the tree. What do you expect the local volatility to be at each node? Display the local volatility tree to confirm your answer.

    d. Display the Arrow-Debreu price tree, and complete the following steps:

        i. Add up all of the nodes at the time step labeled 30 days. The sum should be something less than 1. Why? Write P for this sum.

        ii. Compute

$$e^{0.10 \cdot (30/365) \cdot P}$$

where you computed P in the last exercise. What is the meaning of this expression?

    6. Reconstruct the tree from the previous exercise, and display the distribution of the tree by pressing the DISTRIBUTION button. There is a stock price distribution (left diagram) and a stock return distribution (right diagram). What distributions do these two distributions approximate?

    a. What is the mean of the terminal price distribution? (Hint: The answer has to do with the construction of the tree.)

    b. What is the mean (value) of the stock return distribution?

    7. To make the approximation in the previous example more exact, reconstruct the same tree, but this time with 50 periods. Redisplay the distribution. Why do the new distributions look more like the log-normal and normal distributions?

8. Set

$$S = 100$$
$$T = 30 \text{ days}$$
$$\sigma = 1\%$$
$$r = 50\%$$

Try to build a Cox-Ross-Rubinstein tree with these input parameters. You will get an error message.

    a. Compute the transition probability from the transition probability formula.

    b. Find the minimum interest rate (keeping all of the other parameters fixed) such that you can construct the tree without getting the error message. (Hint: You can either deduce this using the calculator or solve for it directly using the construction of the tree.)

    c. Set the volatility to 3% and repeat the previous question.

Equal Probability Trees
The following questions will reinforce the basic way equal probability trees are built.

    9. Build a five-period equal probability tree with the following data (to build the tree, set the values of the parameters as given, select CRR Tree from the "Option Type" menu, and press EVALUATE OPTION):

$$S = 100$$
$$T = 30 \text{ days}$$
$$\sigma = 15\%$$
$$r = 10\%$$

Answer the following questions:

    a. Display the binomial stock price tree, and verify directly that

$$d = \frac{2e^{\mu \Delta t}}{e^{2\sigma \sqrt{\Delta t}} + 1}$$

$$u = \frac{2e^{\mu \Delta t + 2\sigma \sqrt{\Delta t}}}{e^{2\sigma \sqrt{\Delta t}} + 1}$$

    b. Now use the formula for the transition probabilities to verify that the up and down transition probabilities are equal to 50%.

10. Set

$$S = 100$$
$$T = 30 \text{ days}$$
$$\sigma = 1\%$$
$$r = 50\%$$

Try to build an equal probabilities tree. Did you succeed? Why?

Trees with Lumpy Dividends

11. Enter a single dividend payment of $30 at 20 days into the system. Set

$$S = 100$$
$$T = 30 \text{ days}$$
$$\sigma = 15\%$$
$$r = 10\%$$

Display the tree. The terminal nodes should all be less than $100. What does this reflect economically?

REVIEW QUESTIONS

The following questions pertain to one-period Cox-Ross-Rubinstein trees.

1. Does increasing the risk-free rate of interest (and leaving all other parameters constant) increase or decrease the risk-neutral transition probability of a Cox-Ross-Rubinstein tree?

2. The formula for the local volatility of binomial tree node does not contain any explicit mention of the risk-free rate. Does this mean that local volatility is independent of the risk-free rate?

3. In an equal probabilities tree, the transition probability is always equal to 0.5. How in this case does the risk-free rate influence the local volatility?

4. Use the CRR formulas to produce a one-period tree with parameters set to $S_0 = 100$, $r = 5\%, \sigma = 15\%$, and $\Delta t = 1$ week (i.e. $\Delta t = 1/52$ of a year). Compute the local volatility of the tree. Why is the local volatility not equal to the volatility?

5. What happens to local volatility if you reduce Δt to one day? Does it become closer to the actual volatility? Why? (Make some computations.)

The following problems pertain to large binomial trees and require the computer.

6. Choose values for S, r, σ, and q. Produce a 10-period binomial tree, and record the terminal values of the tree. Produce a bar graph of terminal value versus probability of terminal value. What does the bar graph look like? Do not erase the tree yet.

7. Compute the local volatility at two different nodes of the tree. Why are they the same? What is the local volatility? Why is it not exactly equal to σ?

8. Consider the following Cox-Ross-Rubinstein binomial tree and note the delineated path:

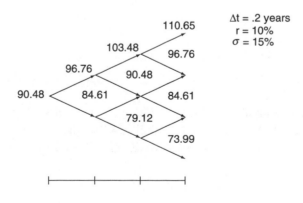

a. What is the probability of traversing the path? (Hint: First compute the up-transition and down-transition probabilities at the vertex node. Next compute the probabilities of each upward or downward movement along the path. Finally, use the notion of independent probabilities to complete the problem.)

b. What is the probability of reaching the final node of the path? (Hint: Count the total number of paths that end up at that node. You may also use the formulas on page 269 of *Black-Scholes and Beyond*.)

9. Compute the up-transition probability at two different nodes of the tree. Are they the same?

10. Keep the same values for S, r, σ, and q as in question 5. Increase the number of periods in the first example to 100, and redo the bar graph. What does the graph look like now? Increase the volatility and repeat the graph. How does the graph change? Do not erase the tree yet.

11. Using the values from the first 10 periods, compute the local volatility of the tree from question 9 at two different nodes. Is it closer to σ than in the case of the 10-period tree?

Arrow-Debreu Prices

12. Construct a three-period binomial tree whose initial date is today and whose final date is one year from today with the following parameters:

$$\sigma = 12\%$$
$$r = 3\%$$

What are the Arrow-Debreu prices of all of the nodes of the tree?

13. Repeat the computation for a 10-period tree, but only compute the final nodes.

14. Call the very top terminal node of the tree and very bottom terminal node of the tree the extreme nodes of the tree. As volatility increases, what happens to the Arrow-Debreu prices of the extreme nodes?

Flexible Trees

15. Consider a one-period binomial tree with vertex node $100, up-node $110, and down-node $90, such as the following:

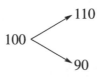

What is the risk-neutral up-transition probability? What is the local volatility of the vertex node of this tree?

16. Now increase the up node to $120, decrease the down node to $80, and recompute both the up-transition probability and the local volatility. What happened, and why? Explain your answers intuitively (See *Black-Scholes and Beyond,* pp. 230–232).

Comparing the Convergence of Cox-Ross-Rubinstein and Equal Probability Trees
    17. Set

$$S = 100$$
$$T = 30 \text{ days}$$
$$\sigma = 15\%$$
$$r = 10\%$$

Complete the following:
    a. Build a 10-period CRR tree, and display the stock price tree. Do not QUIT from the display.
    b. Build a 10-period equal probability tree with the same input parameters as for the CRR tree, and display the stock price tree.
    c. Compare the nodes at various time steps, and get a feel for the average difference between node values for like nodes. For example, compare the top nodes at time step 5 days for each tree.
    d. Now rebuild each type of tree, but this time with 50 periods. Display each tree as in the previous steps. (Note: The Calculator will only display some of the time steps of each tree, but these nodes still correspond to the 50-period tree.) The nodes should be much closer in value. Explain this. What will happen if we move to a 100- or 200-period tree? (Hint: see *Black-Scholes and Beyond* pp. 300-301).
    e. Now compare the transition probability trees for each type of tree at 10 and then 50 periods.
    f. Based on the preceding data, what value do you think the Cox-Ross-Rubinstein transition probabilities converge to when the number of time periods grows to infinity?
It is interesting to note that the preceding logic can be used to prove that any binomial tree that converges to a Brownian motion must have the property that the transition probabilities converge to 50%. Do you think this is true if the tree converges to something other than Brownian motion?

Solutions

Problem 1
We will use the options calculator to answer this question, by building and displaying some binomial trees. By setting the input parameters as follows:

$$S = \$100$$
$$K = \$100$$
$$r = 10\%$$
$$q = 0\%$$
$$T = 30 \text{ days}$$

We now construct a table of interest rates versus transition probabilities by using the options calculator and the following procedure: First, set the input parameters as above. Next, set the *Evaluation Method* to *C-R-R Binomial*. Then set the number of periods to 10. Evaluate the option. Finally, display the transition probability tree.

The pattern is clear: As the risk-free rate increases, so does the transition probability. The reason for this relates to the idea of drift on a stock price process. The risk-free rate determines the upward tendency of the stock price under this process. The larger the risk-free rate, the larger the average value of the stock price under the process. Remember, the average value of a stock price in a binomial is the forward price of the stock, and this is equal to $e^{rT}S$, where S is the vertex node price, and T is equal to the amount of time that passes.

We see, then, that the transition probability is related to the drift of the stock: The greater the drift, the more likely an upward stock price movement.

Problem 2

The formula for local volatility in a Cox-Ross-Rubinstein tree is

$$\sqrt{p(1-P)}\log(S_u/S_d),$$

where $S_u = e^{\sigma\sqrt{\Delta t}}S_0$, and $S_d = e^{-\sigma\sqrt{\Delta t}}S_0$, but the formula for p is

$$p = \frac{e^{r\Delta t} - S_d}{S_u - S_d},$$

so the risk-free rate does influence the local volatility, but only indirectly through the transition probability.

10

⑥ PRICING OPTIONS ON BINOMIAL TREES

REVIEW OF CONCEPTS

In this section we review the basic methods for pricing vanilla European and American options on binomial trees, focusing on Cox-Ross-Rubinstein and equal probability trees. The methods here can be employed for any independent option path at all, but we focus solely on calls and puts.

Pricing a European or American option on a binomial tree proceeds by building an *option pricing tree*. The tree is a companion to the stock price tree. Each node in the option pricing tree represents the price of the option when the stock price is at the price represented by the node. To build the option pricing tree, we proceed in two steps:

1. Price the terminal nodes of the tree.

2. Use backward induction to price nodes prior to the terminal nodes.

Step 1 is the same for both European and American calls and puts. If the option is a call, a terminal node with value S has the value

$$\max(S - K, 0)$$

where K is the strike price of the option. If the option is a call, a terminal node with value S has the value

$$\max(K - S, 0)$$

Once the terminal nodes are valued, we value the set of nodes at the time step directly before the last time step. We will not review this explicitly here since it will be reviewed in detail below.

Hedge Parameters on a Tree

Computing hedge parameters on a tree falls into two distinct categories: hedge parameters that can be read from a tree and hedge parameters that cannot be read from a tree.

Reading a hedge parameter from a tree means building an option pricing tree and using only values from the stock price tree and option tree to compute the hedge parameter.

The values of delta, gamma, and theta can be read directly from the tree (be forewarned, theta can be troublesome in certain instances, see question 6). The values of vega and rho must be estimated using a different method.

The explicit formulas for hedge parameters on a tree will be discussed in question 6.

COMPUTER TUTORIAL

Using the *Black-Scholes and Beyond Interactive Toolkit* to value options on binomial trees is easy. All you need to do is select an option type and an evaluation method, and then set the standard option input parameters to the desired values. When you price an option on a binomial tree using the Options Calculator, the system automatically computes option values and hedge parameters for both the European and American style options you are pricing.

Graphing Option Values

To graph option values using a binomial tree, proceed by entering the option input parameters, and then selecting the evaluation method you wish. Next select the X- and Y-axes from the "Axis" menus, and finally press PLOT X-Z or PLOT X-Y-Z, depending on whether you want a two- or three-dimensional graph.

You may make graphs of option or hedge parameter value versus the number of periods used to build the tree by selecting Periods for the X-axis or Y-axis.

Display Option Pricing Trees

Whenever you evaluate an option using the Options Calculator, a European and an American option pricing tree are created. Moreover, these trees are stored in the system as follows:

1. Each evaluation method separately stores the values of the following types of trees:
   a. Stock price tree.
   b. European option price tree.
   c. American option price tree.
   It also stores enough data to recreate the transition probability tree, local volatility tree, and Arrow-Debreu price tree.
2. Each time you select an evaluation method from the "Evaluation Method" menu, the last set of trees produced by the calculator becomes active.
3. To view an active tree, select the tree you would like to view from the "*Display ...*" pulldown menu, and then press the DISPLAY ... button.
4. You may view as many trees as you like simultaneously from as many different evaluation methods as you like.

QUESTIONS FOR BASIC UNDERSTANDING

Basic Option Pricing on a Tree

1. In this exercise we price both an American and a European put on a Cox-Ross-Rubinstein tree. Set the input parameters as follows:

$$S = \$100$$
$$K = \$100$$
$$T = 1 \text{ year}$$
$$\sigma = 15\%$$
$$r = 10\%$$
$$q = 0\%$$
$$n = 4 \text{ periods}$$

Set the option type to Vanilla Put and the evaluation method to Binomial: CRR. Evaluate the option by pressing the EVALUATE OPTION button. Display the stock price tree, the European option price tree and the American option price tree. Now complete the following exercises:

a. Confirm the value of the terminal nodes of the European and American option tree.

b. Value the bottom node at time $t = 0.75$ in the European option tree. What is the intrinsic value of this node? Is it greater than the value of holding the option?

c. Display the Arrow-Debreu price tree of the option. Compute the sum

$$\sum_{i=0}^{4} \max(K - S_{4,i}, 0) \cdot \lambda_{4,i} \tag{3}$$

where $S_{4,i}$ is the the i'th node from the bottom of the tree at time step 4 and $\lambda_{4,i}$ is the Arrow-Debreu price of the i'th node from the bottom of the Arrow-Debreu of the tree. Why is this sum equal to the European option price?

d. Now compute the sum

$$\sum_{i=0}^{3} \max(K - S_{3,i}, 0) \cdot \lambda_{3,i} \tag{4}$$

Why is this sum also equal to the European option price?

Discussion Pricing options on a binomial tree begins by pricing the terminal nodes of the tree and then successively working backward. Given a two-period tree such as

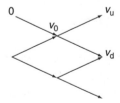

the formula for the value, v_0, of the node labeled 0 is

$$v_0 = e^{-r \cdot \delta t}[pv_u + (1 - p)v_d]$$

where r is the risk-free rate of interest, δt is the length of the time step, p is the up-transition probability from node 0 to node u, and v_u and v_d are the values of the up and down nodes. What this means is that if you are short a contract which requires you to pay v_u if the stock price moves up and v_d if it moves down, then you can hedge this risk at a cost of v_0. Thus, v_0 is the value of node 0 unless there is some exogenous provision for making the value of the node worth more. In the case of American options, there is such a condition: If the intrinsic value of the option at node 0 exceeds the value v_0, then the long position will exercise the right to receive the intrinsic value.

For our tree, set the values of p, r, and Δt to 0.6499, 0.10, and 0.25, respectively. Therefore, the value of the bottom node at time $t = 0.75$ is

$$e^{-0.10 \cdot 0.25}[0.6499 \cdot 13.9292 + (1 - 0.6499) \cdot 25.9182] = 17.6790$$

Note: Do not worry if the preceding values differ in the third or fourth decimal place from the values in the calculator. The calculator computes to a very high precision, whereas the preceding calculation has rounded all the inputs to four decimal places. This accounts for the slight difference in values.

American Option The intrinsic value at the same node is the difference between the strike price and the stock price at that node, which, in this case, is 20.1484. This is greater than 17.6790, so the American version of the option will be exercised.

Arrow-Debreu Prices We know from *Black-Scholes and Beyond* that a European option's value is the discounted expected value of its future price. This is exactly the risk-neutral value of the option, and is the sum of node values times Arrow-Debreu price.

European Options versus Black-Scholes

2. We have learned the following facts in *Black-Scholes and Beyond:*

- Cox-Ross-Rubinstein and equal probability trees are discrete time approximations of geometric Brownian motion. For a given volatility, drift rate (risk-free rate), and dividend yield, the number tree "converges" to a geometric Brownian motion with the same volatility, drift, and dividend yield as the number of periods in a binomial tree increases.
- Pricing a European option on a binomial tree produces a "no-arbitrage" price for the option under the assumption that the underlying stock price follows the binomial tree process.
- Pricing a European option using Black-Scholes produces a "no-arbitrage" price for the option under the assumption that the underlying stock follows a geometric Brownian motion.

These three points lead us to believe that if we increase the number of periods in the trees we use to price options, the prices we obtain will "converge" to Black-Scholes prices. This exercise studies the nature of this convergence.

Complete the following exercises:

a. Set the following parameters on the Options Calculator for a European call option:

$$S = \$100$$
$$K = \$100$$
$$r = 10\%$$
$$q = 0\%$$
$$T = 1 \text{ year}$$
$$\sigma = 15\%$$

b. Make a graph of the call option value (Z-axis) versus number of periods (X-axis) using the PLOT X-Z feature of the Options Calculator. Note the shape of the graph.

c. Now compute the value of the previous 1-year call option with a varying number of periods, and make a table like this one:

	Number of Periods									**Black-Scholes**
	10	20	30	40	50	75	100	150	200	
Option value										

d. Compute the Black-Scholes value of the option to complete the preceding table.

To complete this exercise, repeat the preceding procedure for a call struck at 90 and a call struck at 110, and answer the following questions

	Number of Periods									**Black-Scholes**
	10	20	30	40	50	75	100	150	200	
Option value										

	Number of Periods									**Black-Scholes**
	10	20	30	40	50	75	100	150	200	
Option value										

FIGURE 2

How to Compute the Hedge Parameters Δ, Γ, and Θ from a Binomial tree.

One needs to know the stock prices (denoted by S) and option prices (denoted C).

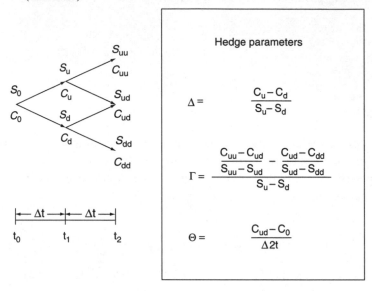

a. What type of option (in-, out-, or at-the-money) converges most rapidly to the Black-Scholes price? That is, which moneyness most "quickly" (i.e., in the least number of periods) produces prices closest to the Black-Scholes price?

b. Continue using the same methodology as given earlier to try and answer this question: Is the convergence rate of a European put option approximately the same as that of a European call on the same underlying with the same expiration and strike? (Hint: Consider put-call parity.)

c. Use your answer to part b to think about part a.

Computing Delta, Gamma, and Theta on a Tree

3. For this exercise we will explicitly go through the steps of computing hedge parameters for a European call option on a tree. Figure 2 displays the formulas for computing hedge parameters on a tree.[1]

Set the Options Calculator input parameters as follows:

$$S = \$100$$
$$K = \$100$$

---

[1]Table 2 corrects an error in Figure 7.6.1 of the first printing of *Black-Scholes and Beyond*. For the correct formula and an explanation, see page 312, formula (7.8.1) of *Black-Scholes and Beyond*.

$$T = 1 \text{ year}$$
$$\sigma = 15\%$$
$$r = 10\%$$
$$q = 0\%$$
$$n = 4 \text{ periods}$$

Complete the following exercises:

a. Value a call option with the preceding parameters on a Cox-Ross-Rubinstein tree.

b. Display the European call option tree and the stock price tree.

c. What are the values S_0, S_u, S_d, S_{uu}, S_{ud}, and S_{dd}?

d. What are the values C_0, C_u, C_d, C_{uu}, C_{ud}, and C_{dd}?

e. Use the formulas in Figure 2 to compute the values of Δ, Γ, and Θ.

Discussion Let's go through the calculation precisely. We have the following chart:

	0	u	d	uu	ud	dd
S	100.0000	107.7883	92.7743	116.1834	100.0000	86.0708
C	11.2750	15.5688	4.1207	21.0605	6.5014	0.0000

Now we compute the hedge parameters:

a. Delta:

$$\frac{C_u - C_d}{S_u - S_d} = \frac{15.5688 - 4.1207}{107.7883 - 92.7743} = 0.7625$$

b. Gamma:

$$\frac{\frac{C_{uu}-C_{ud}}{S_{uu}-S_{ud}} - \frac{C_{ud}-C_{dd}}{S_{ud}-S_{dd}}}{S_u - S_d} = \frac{\frac{21.0605-6.5014}{116.1834-100} - \frac{6.5014-0.0000}{100-86.0708}}{107.7883 - 92.7743} = 0.0288$$

c. Theta:

$$\frac{C_{ud} - C_0}{2 \cdot \Delta t} = \frac{6.5014 - 11.2750}{0.5000} = -9.5472$$

REVIEW QUESTIONS

In the following review questions, set the Options Calculator input parameters as follows:

$$S = \$100$$
$$K = \$100$$
$$T = 1 \text{ year}$$

$$\sigma = 15\%$$
$$r = 10\%$$
$$q = 0\%$$

You may vary the values of the input parameters for further experimentation.

1. Value a vanilla European call with 5-, 10-, and 25-period binomial trees. After each valuation compute the Black-Scholes implied volatility of the resulting option. Write σ_5 for the implied volatility of the option price for the 5-period tree, σ_{10} for the 10-period tree, etc. Answer the following questions:

    a. Each option was evaluated with 15% input volatility. Why are the implied volatilities not equal to 15%?

    b. Now set the number of periods to 100. Evaluate the option, and view the local volatility tree of the stock price tree. The local volatilities will be 14.9978%, but the Black-Scholes implied volatility is still not 14.92%. What does this say about the relationship between binomial tree local volatility and Black-Scholes implied volatility?

2. In *Black-Scholes and Beyond,* page 271, we discussed briefly the relationship between butterfly spreads and Arrow-Debreu prices. We explore that relationship further here. Set the input parameters to the Options Calculator as follows:

$$S = \$100$$
$$T = 1 \text{ year}$$
$$\sigma = 15\%$$
$$r = 10\%$$
$$q = 0\%$$
$$n = 12 \text{ periods}$$

Write

$$K_1 = \quad \$99.50$$
$$K_2 = \$100.00$$
$$K_3 = \$100.50$$

and create three European call options struck at K_1, K_2, and K_3, respectively. Write C_1 for the value of the vanilla call struck at K_1, C_2 for the value of the vanilla call struck at K_2, etc. Then a butterfly spread with strikes K_1, K_2, and K_3 is the combination of two shares of C_1 and C_3 long with one share of C_2 short. We will say that this butterfly spread is centered at K_2. Its value is

$$C_1 - 2 \cdot C_2 + C_3$$

To value this butterfly spread using the Options Calculator, simply set "Option Type" to Butterfly Spread, the Lower Strike to K_1, Strike Price to K_2, and Upper Strike to K_3.

    Complete the following exercises:

    a. Value the European butterfly spread on a 10-period binomial tree (Cox-Ross-Rubinstein or equal probabilities). You may use the Options Calculator directly to create a butterfly spread of call options.

b. Graph the payoff of the butterfly spread versus stock price with no time to expiration (enter a 0 into the Expiry slider display). What is the payoff of the butterfly spread at expiration when the stock price is exactly $100?

3. This exercise explores the different convergence rates of the equal probability and Cox-Ross-Rubinstein trees. Complete the following set of exercises:

a. Set the standard set of input parameters as follows:

$$S = \$100$$
$$K = \$100$$
$$T = 1 \text{ year}$$
$$\sigma = 15\%$$
$$r = 10\%$$
$$q = 0\%$$

Make a graph of call option value versus number of periods using first equal probabilities trees and then the Cox-Ross-Rubinstein trees. What conclusions can you draw from these graphs?

b. Now we will try to see more precisely the relationship between number of periods and option value for each method. Complete the following table:

Number of Periods	CRR Value	EQPR Value	CRR − BS Value	EQPR − BS Value
10	11.5071	11.6063	−0.1625	−0.0633
20				
30				
40				
50				
60				
100				

We have filled in the first row of this table. The first column is the number of periods to use in building the binomial tree. The second and third columns are, respectively, the Cox-Ross-Rubinstein and equal probabilities values of the tree, and the third and fourth columns are the differences between the Cox-Ross-Rubinstein values and the equal probability values, respectively.

c. Now repeat this procedure for options that are in-the-money (strike price 96) and out-of-the-money (strike price 104).

d. What general conclusions can you draw about the convergence properties of the Cox-Ross-Rubinstein versus the equal probability trees?

4. One of the advantages of binomial tree methods over analytic methods is the ability to price American options and compute their hedge parameters. Set the input parameters as follows:

S = $100
K = $99
T = 30 days
σ = 15%
r = 10%
q = 0%
n = 30 periods

Complete the following exercises:

a. Price an American and a European put option.

b. What is the early exercise premium of the American put option?

c. If we move the strike price up a small amount, what will happen to the size of the early exercise premium? Confirm your answer using the Options Calculator. (Note: When we move the strike price up, the values of both the European and American options increase. The question is, do they increase the same amount, or does one increase more than the other?)

d. In general, if the early exercise premium gets larger, will the delta of the American put grow larger or smaller relative to the European put?

e. Is the delta of an American put, in general, greater in magnitude or lesser in magnitude than the corresponding European put? Use the Options Calculator to confirm your answer. What is the intuitive reason for your answer?

5. In this exercise we will study the convergence patterns of the hedge parameters on a binomial tree. Set the input parameters as follows:

S = $100
K = $100
T = 1 year
σ = 15%
r = 10%
q = 0%

Complete the following exercises:

a. Make a graph of call option delta versus number of periods.

b. Make a graph of call option gamma versus number of periods.

c. Make a graph of call option theta versus number of periods.

d. Make a graph of call option vega versus number of periods.

e. Make a graph of call option rho versus number of periods.

f. Repeat these graphs for options that are in- and out-of-the-money.

g. What conclusions can you draw about calculating delta, gamma, and theta on a tree?

h. What general conclusions can you draw about calculating vega and rho on a tree?

6. *Black-Scholes and Beyond,* page 312, points out that, in certain instances, the standard method for deriving theta from a binomial tree can lead to poor results. This exercise illustrates that point.

Set the input parameters as follows:

$$S = \$100$$
$$K = \$112$$
$$T = 1 \text{ year}$$
$$\sigma = 30\%$$
$$r = 1\%$$
$$q = 0\%$$

This set of parameters will lead to negative probabilities in a Cox-Ross-Rubinstein tree, so an equal probabilities tree must be used. We will evaluate a European call option:

a. First evaluate the option using the Black-Scholes formula, and note the theta of the option and the value of the option.

b. Next evaluate the option on a 30-period equal probabilities tree. Note the theta of the option and the value of the option. Is the theta correct? Is the value of the option correct?

c. Now use a 100-period equal probabilities tree. Does this improve the computation?

d. Now apply the formula for Θ on page 312 of *Black-Scholes and Beyond:*

$$\Theta = rC - \left(rS\Delta + \frac{1}{2}\sigma^2 S_0^2 \Gamma\right),$$

where C is the call option value. (Make sure to use the values of Δ and Γ from the tree.)

e. Now experiment with other strike prices, and try to draw some general conclusions about the estimation value of the two formulas for theta.

7. Set the input parameters as follows:

$$S = \$100$$
$$K = \$100$$
$$r = 10\%$$
$$q = 0\%$$

Value the preceding option for two weeks, six months, and one year to expiration, with volatilities of 10%, 15%, and 25%, in the following ways:

• With a 25-period Cox-Ross-Rubinstein tree.
• With a 100-period Cox-Ross-Rubinstein tree.
• With the Black-Scholes formula.

Also, make a graph of number of periods versus option value (on a Cox-Ross-Rubinstein tree) for each option.

Answer the following questions:

a. How does increasing stock price volatility affect the convergence of Cox-Ross-Rubinstein tree option values to Black-Scholes values?

    b. How does increasing time to expiry affect the convergence of Cox-Ross-Rubinstein tree option values to Black-Scholes values?

    c. What is the intuitive explanation for these results?

Solutions

Problem 1

    a. The implied volatilities are not equal to 15 percent because the options were valued on a binomial tree and then the implied volatility was produced using the Black-Scholes formula. Remember, the Black-Scholes implied volatility computes the volatility in the Black-Scholes formula that will produce a given option price. Since the Cox-Ross-Rubinstein binomial tree price of an option with 15 percent volatility is only an approximation of the Black-Scholes price, we cannot expect the implied volatility to be exactly 15 percent. This is another way of seeing that the Cox-Ross-Rubinstein price is only an approximation of the Black-Scholes price.

    b. Binomial tree local volatility is used to produce an option price. This option price then produces a Black-Scholes implied volatility which is different from the local volatility. This points to the fact that binomial trees are only approximating Brownian motion, and there are errors in this approximation.

11

⑥   IMPLIED VOLATILITY TREES

This chapter differs slightly in form from the earlier chapters in this book. There is not a long list of questions about implied trees but rather a small series of discussions about various aspects concerning their use. We focus on the basic principles of implied trees, their construction and convergence properties, as well as their relation with the volatility smile. We will see the use of pricing barrier options with implied trees in Chapter 12 later in this book.

REVIEW OF CONCEPTS

An implied volatility tree is a binomial tree constructed using as inputs a set of option prices. The implied volatility tree prices the set of input options according to the input prices. The mathematical motivation for the trees is to find a set of local volatilities for the diffusion process that controls the underlying stock movement, which prices all the input options correctly. The financial economic motivation is to build a model, unlike Black-Scholes, that prices options according to a market and use the resulting model (the tree) to price options not traded in the market and build hedge parameters for the traded options.

Construction of Trees

The following is a summary of *Black-Scholes and Beyond*, pp. 385–90. In this summary we do not discuss the construction of implied volatility trees for American input options but instead refer you to *Black-Scholes and Beyond*, Chapter 9.

The Setup

To build an implied volatility tree we start with a set of input data. The following is the list of data we need:

1. An underlying stock or index, S, with a fixed spot price for today's date, denoted S_0.

2. A set of input options on S. For this chapter we assume the input data are a set of European options. We assume that, for each option, we know its strike price, its type (call or put), and its price. For example, if our underlying is the S&P 500, we would want the price of every traded European option on the S&P 500.

Given this input data, we will build the following output data one time step at a time:

1. A stock price tree.

2. An Arrow-Debreu price tree.

Along the way we will need a method for interpolating option prices. In our method and in the *Black-Scholes and Beyond Interactive Toolkit* Options Calculator, we use bilinear interpolation.

Notation

We will use the following notation in this section.

$$
\begin{aligned}
t_0, t_1, \ldots, t_n &= \text{time steps of the tree.} \\
r_i &= \text{the forward interest rate applying from time } t_{i-1} \text{ to } t_i. \\
D_i &= \text{dividend payment for ex-date } t_i. \\
S_{i,j} &= \text{stock price value of node } (i, j). \\
\lambda_{i,j} &= \text{Arrow-Debreu price of node } (i, j). \\
P(t_i, K) &= \text{market price of a European put option on } S \text{ struck at } K, \text{ expiring at} \\
&\quad \text{time } t_i. \\
C(t_i, K) &= \text{market price of a European call option on } S \text{ struck at } K, \text{ expiring at} \\
&\quad \text{time } t_i. \\
v^{put}_{i-1,j} &= \text{value of } P(t_i, S_{i-1,j}) \text{ at node } (i - 1, j). \\
v^{call}_{i-1,j} &= \text{value of } C(t_i, S_{i-1,j}) \text{ at node } (i - 1, j).
\end{aligned}
$$

Building the Implied Volatility Tree

Filling in the stock price tree proceeds in several steps. The first thing that must be decided is the centering condition of the tree. There are two centering conditions available in the *Black-Scholes and Beyond Interactive Toolkit* Options Calculator: centering at the spot and centering at the forward. The centering condition controls the relationship between the center node of each time step and the vertex node of the tree [recall that the vertex node is node (0,0), the node that represents the initial spot price of the tree]. Centering at the spot price means that the center node will always have the same value as the vertex node. Centering at the forward means that the center node will always have the same value as the forward price (from the initial time of the tree to the current time).

We start by assuming that we have computed all time steps through time step t_{i-1}. This is possible, of course, because we know the value of the nodes at time t_0: there is only one, the spot price. Thus, we take as the starting point we wish to compute, the nodes at time t_i. We now use the following steps.

Step 1—Starting the Time Step

We are at time step t_i, and no nodes are known, so how do we start? We start one of two ways, depending on whether the number of nodes in the time step are even or odd.

When the Number of Nodes Is Odd

If the number of nodes in the time step is odd, then there is a middle node, and we can simply declare the value of this node to be the spot price of the underlying. This builds a tree that looks like a Cox-Ross-Rubinstein tree, where all the middle nodes are equal to the spot price. Note if we were centering at the forward, we would set the middle node to the forward value of the spot price at that time.

If centering at the spot,

$$S_{i,i/2} = S_0 \tag{5}$$

If centering at the forward,

$$S_{i,i/2} = S_0 e^{r_i \Delta t} \tag{6}$$

When the Number of Nodes Is Even

If the number of nodes is even, the time step's number itself is odd, and we need to compute the values of nodes $[i, (i + 1)/2]$ and $[i, (i - 1)/2]$.[1]

Step (a) Compute the value of $v_{i-1,(i-1)/2}^{put}$. To do this we need the value of a put option struck at $S_{i-1,(i-1)/2}$ and expiring at time t_i.

The auxiliary equation. To begin with we use the input smile to interpolate an implied volatility for an option struck at $S_{i-1,i-1}$ and expiring at time t_i. Next, using this volatility, we compute

$$P(t_i, S_{i-1,i-1})$$

the value of a put expiring at time t_i and struck at $S_{i-1,(i-1)/2}$. We compute this value either with the Black-Scholes formula or with a binomial tree.

Once we have $P[t_i, S_{i-1,(i-1)/2}]$ we use it to compute the value $v_{i-1,(i-1)/2}^{put}$ with the following formula:

$$v_{i-1,(i-1)/2}^{put} = \frac{P(t_i, S_{i-1,(i-1)/2}) - \Sigma}{\lambda_{i-1,(i-1)/2}}$$

$$\Sigma = \sum_{k=0}^{i-1} \lambda_{i-1,k}(e^{-r_i \Delta t} S_{i-1,(i-1)/2} - S_{i-1,j} + e^{-r_i \Delta t} D_i) \tag{7}$$

---

[1]This section corrects a small number of errors in *Black-Scholes and Beyond*, (first printing) pp. 386–88 regarding the numbering of the center node. The equations in this section differ in this regard from the equations there. The equations here are correct; we apologize for the inconvenience.

Step (b) If we have completed step a, then we have a value for $v_{i-1,(i-1)/2}^{put}$. Given this, proceed by setting

$$u = \frac{v_{i-1,(i-1)/2}^{put} + S_{i-1,(i-1)/2}}{e^{-r_i\Delta t}S_{i-1,(i-1)/2} - v_{i-1,j}^{put}} \tag{8}$$

and compute $S_{i,(i+1)/2}$ according to the chosen centering condition.

For centering at the spot price, we set

$$\begin{aligned} S_{i,(i+1)/2} &= S_{i-1,(i-1)/2}u \\ S_{i,(i-1)/2} &= S_{i-1,(i-1)/2}/u \end{aligned} \tag{9}$$

For centering at the forward, we set

$$\begin{aligned} S_{i,(i+1)/2} &= S_{i-1,(i-1)/2}u \\ S_{i,(i-1)/2} &= [S_{i-1,(i-1)/2}e^{r_i\Delta t}]/u \end{aligned} \tag{10}$$

Step (c) Now we compute the up transition probability, $p_{i-1,(i-1)/2}$, from node $[i-1, (i-1)/2]$ to node $[i, (i+2)/2]$. In this case, we compute

$$p_{i-1,(i-1)/2} = \frac{e^{r_i\Delta t}S_{i-1,(i-1)/2} - D_i - S_{i,(i-1)/2}}{S_{i,(i+1)/2} - S_{i,(i-1)/2}} \tag{11}$$

Step 2—Moving Down the Tree

Assume we are at time step t_i, and suppose we have just computed the value of node $S_{i,j+1}$, where $S_{i,j+1}$ is below the middle of the tree. We now want to compute the value of node $S_{i,j}$, the next node down. We proceed again in three steps.

Step (a) First we determine the value of $v_{i-1,j}^{put}$. To do this we need the value of a put option struck at $S_{i-1,j}$, expiring at time t_i.

We use the bilinear interpolation method to produce a value for $P(t_i, S_{i-1,j})$. To compute $v_{i-1,j}^{put}$ we use the following formula:

$$\begin{aligned} v_{i-1,j}^{put} &= \frac{P(t_i, S_{i-1,j}) - \Sigma}{\lambda_{i-1,j}} \\ \Sigma &= \sum_{k=0}^{j-1} \lambda_{i-1,k}(e^{-r_i\Delta t}S_{i-1,j} - S_{i-1,k} + e^{-r_i\Delta t}D_i) \end{aligned} \tag{12}$$

Step (b) We now have a value for $v_{i-1,j}^{put}$, and we are ready to compute the value of $S_{i,j}$. For this we use the formula

$$S_{i,j} = \frac{v_{i-1,j}^{put}S_{i,j+1} + (S_{i-1,j} - e^{-r_i\Delta t}S_{i,j+1})S_{i-1,j}}{v_{i-1,j}^{put} + S_{i-1,j} - e^{-r_i\Delta t}S_{i,j+1}} \tag{13}$$

Once we have done this we continue to move down the tree until all of the nodes below the middle node(s) have been filled in.

Step (c) We now compute the transition probability, $p_{i-1,j}$ from node $(i-1, j)$ to node $(i, j+1)$. We have

$$p_{i-1,j} = \frac{e^{r_i \Delta t} S_{i-1,j} - D_i - S_{i,j}}{S_{i,j+1} - S_{i,j}}$$

Step 3—Moving Up the Tree

We are at time step t_i. Suppose we have just computed the value of node $S_{i,j}$, where $S_{i,j}$ lies above the center of the tree. We now want to compute the value of node $S_{i,j+1}$. Once again we proceed in three steps.

Step (a) First determine the value of $v_{i-1,j}^{\text{put}}$. To do this we need the value of a call option struck at $S_{i-1,j}$, expiring at time t_i.

The auxiliary equation. In this case the input option is European, and we use bilinear interpolation to produce a value for $C(t_i, S_{i-1,j})$.

$$v_{i-1,j}^{call} = \frac{C(t_i, S_{i-1,j}) - \Sigma}{\lambda_{i-1,j}}$$

$$\Sigma = \sum_{k=j+1}^{i} \lambda_{i-1,k}(S_{i-1,k} - e^{-r_i \Delta t} S_{i-1,j} - e^{-r_i \Delta t} D_i)$$

(14)

Step (b) We now have a value for $v_{i-1,j}^{put}$, and we have to compute the value of $S_{i,j+1}$. For this we set

$$S_{i,j+1} = \frac{v_{i-1,j}^{call} S_{i,j} + (e^{-r_i \Delta t} S_{i,j} - S_{i-1,j}) S_{i-1,j}}{v_{i-1,j}^{call} + e^{-r_i \Delta t} S_{i,j} - S_{i-1,j}}$$

(15)

Step (c) We now compute the transition probability $p_{i-1,j}$ to $p_{i,j+1}$:

$$p_{i-1,j} = \frac{e^{r_i \Delta t} S_{i-1,j} - D_i - S_{i,j}}{S_{i,j+1} - S_{i,j}}$$

Bad Transition Probabilities

If the transition probability $p_{l,m}$ is less than 0 or greater than 1 in any of the preceding computations, the probability is deemed bad, and the node computation cannot be used. In this case the node must be physically removed and replaced by a node that produces a good probability. There is no "correct" mathematical way to do this; instead we content ourselves with several possible choices for making these computations. See *Black-Scholes and Beyond* (pp. 379–384) for more details.

COMPUTER TUTORIAL

The following is a guide to using the *Black-Scholes and Beyond Interactive Toolkit* Options Calculator to enter volatility smiles and build implied volatility trees from them. Once an implied volatility tree is built, it is "in the system" and can be used to price as many options as you wish.

Entering a Volatility Smile

Entering a volatility smile into the system is easy. The first step is to create a list of option-implied volatilities and arrange them by strike and expiration. You can have the expiries in units of days, weeks, months, or years.

To enter a smile into the Options Calculator complete the following steps:

1. From the Main Screen pull down the "Evaluation Method" menu and select Implied Volatility. A button should pop up labeled BUILD TREE.

2. Click the BUILD TREE button. A screen will pop up: Smile Entry Data. From this screen you will enter the number of strikes in your smile and the number of expirations. Enter each number in the appropriate box and click the pushbutton labeled ENTER SMILE. If you change your mind and do not want to enter a smile, click the button labeled CANCEL.

3. If you click ENTER SMILE, the Smile Entry Data screen will close and a screen labeled Black-Scholes and Beyond Toolkit: Smile Input Screen will pop up. The screen has the following properties:

    a. There is a matrix of cells in the center for entering implied volatilities. This is called the smile matrix.

    b. The number of rows in the smile matrix is equal to the number of expiries you chose in the Smile Entry Data screen.

    c. The number of columns in the smile matrix is equal to the number of strikes you chose in the Smile Entry Data screen.

    d. Along the left side of the matrix is a column of cells for entering expiration dates.

    e. Along the upper row of the matrix is a row for entering strikes.

4. Each cell of the smile entry matrix should be filled with the implied volatility of an option with expiry corresponding to its row and strike corresponding to its column.

5. To enter a strike price, click in a box in the top row of the screen, and enter the strike in dollars. You may enter as many digits of precision as you like.

6. To enter an expiration date, click in a box on the left column of the screen, and enter the expiration date measured in the amount of time from today. The units of the expiration date are noted at the top of the screen. For example, if the units are in days, the top of the screen will read

    Expiry in Days . . . strike in dollars

You may change the expiry units if you like. (See "Editing a Smile" for information on this.)

7. To enter an implied volatility, click the left mouse in any cell of the smile input matrix, and enter the implied volatility in percentages. For example, if you wish to enter an implied volatility of 15.34%, enter the number 15.34 into the appropriate cell.

8. When you are done entering the smile you may do one of three things:

    a. To save the smile and quit, click SAVE SMILE. This will store the smile you just entered into the system for later use and close the screen.

b. To quit and delete the smile, click QUIT. This will delete the smile you just entered and close the screen.

c. To build an implied volatility tree, click BUILD TREE. This will build an implied volatility tree with the smile you just entered.

Using the Automated Fill Features

There are two features available for entering simple smiles. They are accessed by pressing either of the two buttons from the Smile Input screen:

1. FLAT FILL.
2. CEV FILL.

Flat Fill

When you click the FLAT FILL button, a screen appears that will look something like this:

Strike:	From:	*	To:	*
Expiry:	From:	*	To:	*
Vol:	From:	*	To:	*

The asterisks in the table mean that some value will appear, but the value depends on the particulars of your session. Each box with an asterisk requires you to fill in a value.

1. Strike. Enter a range of strikes from low to high. This tells the Options Calculator to fill the row of strikes in the Smile Input matrix from the "From" value evenly up to the "To" value.

2. Expiry. Enter a range of expiries from low to high in the units displayed in the Smile Entry screen. This tells the Options Calculator to fill the column of expiries in the Smile Input matrix from the "From" value evenly up to the "To" value.

3. Vol. The four Volatility values tell the Options Calculator what the volatility values in the "corners" of the Smile Input matrix will be. The idea is that from these corner values and the amount of variation of the strikes and expiries, the Options Calculator can fill in the rest of the smile matrix.

When you are done entering these values, press the FILL button. This will fill the volatility matrix.

CEV FILL

The CEV FILL feature allows you to fill in the volatility smile matrix with implied volatilities computed from the CEV model of volatility movements.

The CEV FILL allows the user to automatically enter a volatility smile of the form

$$\sigma(K, t) = \sigma_0 \cdot (K/S)^{\beta}(t + 1)^{\alpha}$$

That is, the implied volatility of an option with strike K and expiry t is given by the above formula, where σ_0, β and α are parameters determined by the user. In general, CEV models $(t + 1)^{\alpha}$ may be replaced by arbitrary functions of time, i.e., the CEV model may have the form

$$\sigma(K, t) = \sigma_0 \cdot (K/S)^\beta f(t),$$

but the Toolkit limits itself to the simpler form above. Another thing to note is that usually CEV models refer to the structure of local volatility, not implied volatility. However, since we are studying implied volatility, we simply transport the CEV formula to implied volatility and study it in that context.

To enter a CEV smile into the Options Calculator, proceed in the following steps:

- From the Toolkit Smile Input screen click on the CEV FILL button. A screen titled "CEV Fill Screen" will pop up.
- You may enter each of the parameter values σ_0, β and α by either clicking the left mouse button over corresponding display or adjusting the slider to the right of the display.
    - **To enter σ_0:** Enter a value in the row labeled *Base vol (%)*
    - **To enter β:** Enter a value in the row *Beta*
    - **To enter α:** Enter a value in the row *Alpha*
- To fill the volatility matrix with CEV model, click on FILL.
- To quit the CEV FILL Screen without filling the volatility, click on *Dismiss*.

Editing a Volatility Smile

There are two main reasons for editing a smile:

1. While building a smile, you realize you want to alter something about the smile you are building.
2. There is a smile in the system you want to change in some way.

All volatility smile editing takes place in the Smile Input screen. There are three main ways to edit the smile:

1. Insert a row or column from the matrix. The Options Calculator allows you to add as many rows or columns as you wish before or after any given row and fill the new rows with a specified value. To insert a row or column, proceed as follows:

    a. From the Smile Input screen, pull down the "Insert . . . " menu.

    b. Select Row or Column.

    c. If, for example, you wish to insert a number of rows, you will be prompted for the following information:

        i. Starting row.

        ii. Number of rows.

        iii. Insert value.

        iv. Before/after.

Starting row refers to the row number at which you wish to insert the new row(s). Rows are numbered from the top down; that is, row 1 is the top row. Now you must decide if you wish to insert the rows *before* the starting row or *after* the starting row. The Options Calculator will do either. To select the position desired, press the button next to "Before/After." This toggles between before and after.

      d. When you are done entering these data, either press OK or CANCEL.

      e. Clicking the OK button will close both the Insert ... screen and the Smile Input screen and then redraw the Smile Input screen with the appropriate number of rows or columns inserted.

      2. Delete a row or column from the matrix. To delete rows from the Smile Input matrix, pull down the "Delete ..." menu from the Smile Input screen and select Row or Column. In the case of deleting a number of rows, a screen will pop up labeled "Delete Row," which prompts you for the following information:

      a. Starting row.

      b. Number of rows.

Starting row is the row you want to delete first, counted from the top down (i.e., row 1 is the top row). You may press OK or CANCEL. If you press OK, the Options Calculator will delete from the Smile Input matrix the number of rows specified, starting with the row you specify.

      3. Sort a row or column in ascending order.

      You may sort the row or column headers of the Smile Entry Matrix by pulling down the Sort ... menu at the top of the screen. There are two options:

      a. Rows: sorts the rows from nearest expiry (toward the top of the screen) to furthest expiry (toward the bottom of the screen).

      b. Columns: sorts the columns from least strike level (toward the left of the screen) to greatest strike level (toward the right of the screen).

Plotting the volatility smile

You may produce a three-dimensional graph of the current implied volatility tree in the system using the following steps:

    1. From the main Options Calculator screen, open the Smile Input screen by pressing either the BUILD TREE button or the VIEW/EDIT SMILE button.

    2. In the Smile Input screen, make sure the smile in the input matrix is the smile you want to plot.

    3. From the Smile Input screen, press the PLOT SMILE button.

After pressing the PLOT SMILE button, a three-dimensional graph of the smile will pop up. The graph is a graph of strike price and expiration versus Black-Scholes implied volatility.

Building an Implied Volatility Tree

Once you have a volatility smile in the system, you can use the smile to build an implied volatility tree. To build the tree you have to first enter the volatility smile into the system and then set the various input parameters to the tree. We summarize this procedure here:

1. Enter a volatility smile into the system.

2. Choose a centering condition by clicking the button labeled CENTER SPOT or CEN-TER FORWARD. Clicking the button toggles between the two values. If the button displays CENTER SPOT, the Options Calculator will center at the spot. If the button displays CENTER FORWARD, the Options Calculator will center at the forward.

3. Select the type of underlying to price using the "Underlying type" pull-down menu.

4. Set the current stock price (currency spot rate or futures price) using the Stock Price (Spot rate or Futures price) slider display.

5. Set the current risk-free rate of interest using the Risk-Free Rate slider display.

6. Choose a time-length for the tree by setting the Expiry slider display. For example, if you want a one-year long implied volatility tree, first set the tree units to years (use the "Options" menu) and then set expiry display to 1 (year).

7. Set the current dividend yield using the Div'd Yield slider display, or enter a dividend schedule by depressing the ENTER DIV'DS button.

8. Choose the number of periods for the implied volatility tree using the Periods slider display.

9. From the Smile Input screen click the BUILD TREE button. This will read the current set of input parameters from the currently open screens: It will read in the current smile and read in the current stock price, risk-free rate and dividend schedule.

10. Keep in mind that you may build implied volatility trees for any type of underlying you wish, simply by setting UNDERLYING TYPE.

Computing Option Prices Using Implied Volatility Trees

Once an implied volatility tree has been built, it remains in the system as long as the Options Calculator is up. You can price options using any of the other methods and return to the implied tree later to price other options. You can even price with the implied tree, then with a different kind of tree, and still return to pricing with the implied tree. To price an option with an implied tree, proceed as follows:

1. Build an implied volatility tree using the procedure outlined earlier on pp. 88–89.

2. Set the option type by pulling down the "Option Type" menu to the appropriate type of option.

3. Pull down the "Evaluation Method" menu, and select Implied Volatility. It does not matter if you have priced options using other trees since you build the tree.

4. Set the underlying type by pulling down the "Underlying Type" menu.

5. Set the input parameters of strike price, risk-free rate, dividend payments, expiry, etc., using the appropriate slider displays.

6. Set the barrier level if the option is a barrier-type option.

7. *Do not set stock price or periods.* When you evaluate an option on an implied tree, the Options Calculator automatically sets these parameters to the values appropriate for the current implied volatility tree in the system. For example, if the implied volatility tree in the system is

50 periods and has an initial stock price of $100, when you evaluate an option using this tree, the Calculator will automatically set the periods to 50 and the stock price to $100.

8. Evaluate the option by clicking the EVALUATE OPTION button.

When you evaluate an option using an implied volatility tree, the following are computed:

- The European value of the option and all its Greeks.
- The American option value and all its Greeks.

These values are displayed in the upper-right portion of the Calculator Display.

Displaying Implied Distributions

After you have built an implied volatility tree, you may display its implied distribution using the Options Calculator. To do so, do as follows:

1. Set "Evaluation Method" to Implied Volatility.

2. Set the input parameters of stock price, interest rate, dividend yield, expiry, etc.

3. Enter a volatility smile into the system from the Smile Input screen.

4. Build the implied volatility tree by clicking BUILD TREE from the Smile Input screen.

5. Click the DISTRIBUTION button in the main screen.

A Note on Interpolation

The *Black-Scholes and Beyond Interactive Toolkit* Options Calculator uses the following basic rules for interpolation:

1. If the input smile has only one expiration time, linear interpolation is used to compute implied volatilities between strikes.

2. If the input smile has only one strike price, linear interpolation is used to compute implied volatilities between expirations.

3. If bilinear interpolation does occur, values outside the range of the smile are interpolated using the following algorithm:

    a. If the input strike is greater than (less than) the greatest (least) strike, then the input strike is set to the greatest (least) strike before interpolation.

    b. If the input expiration is longer than (shorter than) the longest (shortest) expiration, then the input expiration is set to the longest (shortest) expiration.

QUESTIONS FOR BASIC UNDERSTANDING

In the following questions we will build some implied volatility trees from a set of input options and study the details of the process. In addition, we will learn about the economic and market significance of pricing on trees as well as bad probabilities and bilinear interpolation.

1. In this example, we will build a two-period tree and check the accuracy of the *Black-Scholes and Beyond Interactive Toolkit* Options Calculator. Start with the following input data:

$$S_{0,0} = \$100$$
$$r = 10\%$$
$$\Delta t = 1 \text{ year}$$

We are going to build a two-period tree, so we need to set the expiry equal to two years. In this example, we are going to use the no-smile smile; that is, we are going to use a constant volatility input smile of 15%. Once we have built the tree, we will compare its local volatility structure to that of Cox-Ross-Rubinstein trees and equal probability trees.

Proceed in the following steps:

    a. Enter a constant smile into the calculator.

    b. Build a two-period implied volatility tree using this smile.

    c. Display the tree and compare your answers with the answers in the display at time equal to one year.

Build Time Step 1

We have to use step 1, on p. 89, "Starting the Time Step." The number of nodes in this time step is two and therefore is even. We use steps (a) and (b) as described on pp. 89–90. Here is the data we currently know:

$$t_0 = \text{known time step}$$
$$S_{0,0} = \$100 \text{ (known stock price value)}$$
$$\lambda_{0,0} = 1.0 \text{ (known Arrow-Debreu price)}$$

We need to compute:

    a. $P(t_1, S_{0,0})$ = value of European put $S_{0,0}$.

Your task is to compute the value of $P(t_1, S_{0,0})$ using the Black-Scholes formula for European puts. Remember to use the correct input volatility. (Answer: \$2.1533, use 15% input volatility)

    b. Compute the value of $v_{0,0}^{put}$ using Eq. (7). (Answer: \$2.1533) Why is this value the same as the previous step?

    c. Compute the value of u in Eq. (8). (Answer: 1.1564903)

    d. Compute the values of $S_{1,1}$ and $S_{1,0}$ using Eqs. (9). (Answer: $S_{1,1} = 115.6490$ and $S_{1,0} = 86.4685$)

Check these results against the Options Calculator as follows:

    a. Compute the up transition probability from node (0, 0) to node (1, 1) using Eq. (11). In this case, the equation reads

$$p_{0,0} = \frac{e^{0.10}100 - 86.4685}{115.6490 - 86.4685}$$

Check your answer with the Options Calculator.

b. Now compute $\lambda_{1,1}$ and $\lambda_{1,0}$, the Arrow-Debreu prices of nodes $(1, 1)$ and $(1, 0)$, respectively,

    i. The value of $\lambda_{1,1}$ is the probability of reaching node $(1, 1)$ discounted to time t_0.

    ii. The value of $\lambda_{1,0}$ is the probability of reaching node $(1, 0)$ discounted to time t_0.

Check your answers with the Options Calculator's Arrow-Debreu prices.

Building Time Step 2

We continue and build time step t_2 of our implied volatility tree:

1. The number of nodes in this time step is three and, therefore, odd. Thus, according to Eq. (5) we set $S_{2,1}$ equal to \$100.

2. We now move down the tree and compute the value of $S_{2,0}$ in the following steps:

    a. First compute the value of $P(t_2, S_{1,0})$; that is, find the value of a European put option expiring at time t_2 struck at $S_{1,0}$. Use the Black-Scholes formula to make this computation. (What input volatility do you use?)

    b. Next, compute $v_{1,0}^{put}$ using Eq. (12).

    c. Finally, use Eq. (13) to determine the value of $S_{2,0}$. Compare your answer to the one given by the Options Calculator.

3. Now move up the tree and compute the value of $S_{2,2}$.

4. We now address the issue of constant volatility and implied volatility trees. What happens if we enter the no smile smile into an implied volatility tree? That is, what happens if we build an implied tree in which every input option has the same volatility?

First we build the implied volatility tree with the following steps:

    a. Set the following input parameters in the *Black-Scholes and Beyond Interactive Toolkit* Options Calculator:

$$S = \$100$$
$$r = 10\%$$
$$q = 0\%$$
$$T = 3 \text{ months}$$

    b. Input a single expiration of 10 days and a single strike of \$100 into the smile entry data screen.

    c. Build an implied volatility tree with 10 periods.

    d. Do not exit the calculator.

Now we want to see how it prices options and compare the prices to the Black-Scholes prices of options with 10% volatility.

Set the Volatility slider display to 10%, and price the following options using both Black-Scholes and the implied volatility trees model:

Expirations	Strikes			
	90	100	110	120
10 days	/	/	/	/
30 days	/	/	/	/
60 days	/	/	/	/

In each space, record both the Black-Scholes price and the Implied Volatility tree price (optionally, record some of the Greeks as well).

Now repeat the calculation, this time using a tree of 40 periods. Once again record your answers in the following box.

Expirations	Strikes			
	90	100	110	120
10 days	/	/	/	/
30 days	/	/	/	/
60 days	/	/	/	/

Discussion I

The implied volatility tree above was built with every input Black-Scholes implied volatility equal to 10%. As a consequence, we would ideally like every option priced by the tree to have an implied volatility of 10%. This would, in fact, be the case if the tree had an infinitely large number of nodes. Since the tree has only a finite number of nodes, the accuracy of the tree depends on the particular option you price.

If you choose to price an option whose strike price is represented by a node on the tree, then the option should be priced identically to Black-Scholes. This does not always happen, however, because in large trees, bad probabilities come up.

Discussion II—Cox-Ross-Rubinstein Tree Comparison

We will now build a Cox-Ross-Rubinstein tree with 10% volatility and compare its structure with that of the implied volatility tree we build above. Complete the following steps:

    a. Display the 40-period implied volatility tree.
    b. Select Binomial Tree: CRR from the "Evaluation method" menu.
    c. Set the Volatility slider display to 10%.

d. Set the Expiry display to 3 months.

e. Set the number of periods to 40.

f. Depress the EVALUATE OPTION button.

g. Display the stock price tree by select Stock price in the "DISPLAY . . ." menu and depressing the DISPLAY . . . button.

Note that the implied volatility tree and the Cox-Ross-Rubinstein tree are quite different, yet they produce very similar option prices. To understand the meaning of these differences do the following:

h. Display the terminal distribution of both the implied volatility tree and the Cox-Ross-Rubinstein tree.

i. Display the local volatility tree of both the implied volatility tree and the Cox-Ross-Rubinstein tree.

3. This question examines the notion of bad probabilities. We will examine a real example of bad probabilities by reproducing an example from *Black-Scholes and Beyond.*

We will work with the simple smile example on pp. 391–96 of *Black-Scholes and Beyond.* In this example the stock does not pay dividends. As a first step we enter this smile into the system:

a. The volatility smile we want to use has the following form. It is the same for all expirations, and

$$\sigma_{imp} = -K/20 + 20 \quad \text{if } K \leq 110$$

$$\sigma_{imp} = -K/10 + 25.5 \quad \text{if } K \geq 110$$

To enter this smile into the Options Calculator, proceed as follows:

i. Select Implied Volatility from the "Evaluation Method." A button labeled BUILD TREE will appear.

ii. Press the BUILD TREE button. A screen will appear prompting you to enter the number of strikes and number of expiries.

iii. Enter 3 strikes and 1 expiries, and press OK. The current screen will disappear, and a new screen will appear prompting you to enter the smile.

iv. Enter strikes of 80, 110, and 120 and corresponding volatilities of 16, 14.5, and 13.5. These three volatilities completely determine our smile.

Next, we set the parameters for building our tree. We want a tree with four time periods, four years to expiration (i.e., $\Delta t = 1$ year), a 5% risk-free rate of interest, and an initial stock price of $100. Moreover, the tree in *Black-Scholes and Beyond,* p. 395, was produced evaluating options with Cox-Ross-Rubinstein trees. Therefore, we have to set the "Implied Tree" menu to Cox-Ross-Rubinstein. After setting these parameters, return to the Smile Input screen and press BUILD TREE.

Display the stock price tree. If you have done everything correctly, a four-period tree will appear with time in years starting at 0.0 year and displaying times through 4.0 years.

b. At time step t_4 (time = 4.0 years) there is a small white sliver in the second node from the bottom. This sliver indicates that this is a bad node. This indicates that there was a bad probability at this node.

c. Compare this node's value with the value of the node in *Black-Scholes and Beyond* Figure 9.7.2. The node value is different because a different method for replacing bad nodes was used in the book than in the Options Calculator. What sorts of effects on option pricing will this have?

d. Verify that node (4,1) produces a bad probability by using the procedure for computing implied trees to compute the actual node value:

i. Use Step 2—Moving Down the Tree on p. 395. We start by computing the auxiliary value Σ:

$$\Sigma = \sum_{k=0}^{j-1} \lambda_{i-1,k}(e^{-r\Delta t}S_{i-1,j})$$

Note that we have eliminated dividends from the preceding equations because we assume there are no dividend payments. You can use the Options Calculator Arrow-Debreu tree display to help make the computations. (Answer: 0.9832)

ii. Next, compute the value of $P(t_4, S_{3,1})$. To do this, proceed in two steps:

- First compute the correct implied volatility for this option. (Answer: $\sigma = 15.7168\%$)
- Next, use a four-period Cox-Ross-Rubinstein tree to evaluate this option. [Answer: $P(t_4, S_{3,1}) = \$8.68$]

iii. Now put it all together to compute the value of $v_{3,1}^{put}$. (Answer: $v_{3,1}^{put} = 39.8983$)

iv. Use Eq. (13) to compute the value of $S_{4,1}$. (Answer: $S_{4,1} = \$104.4550$)

The conclusion is that the value the implied volatility tree algorithm produces is not valid, for it is greater than the node above it. In such cases, we have to employ an algorithm for replacing the bad node with a good node.

4. This exercise illustrates the original purpose of implied volatility trees: to price a set of input options according to the market. This smile will take a set of four input options and build an implied volatility tree that prices these options correctly.

Table 2 displays our mini-smile consisting of the implied volatilities of four options.

TABLE 2

Implied Volatilities for a
Hypothetical "Mini" Smile

Expiry	Strike	
	90	110
8 months	13.2	12.3
4 months	12.4	11.4

We will build a tree using the following set of data:

$$S = 100$$
$$T = 1 \text{ year}$$
$$r = 10\%$$
$$n = 5$$

Complete the following exercises:

    a. Build an implied volatility tree using the Options Calculator with the preceding data.

    b. Display the tree.

    c. Price the input options used to create the tree. We do this as follows:

        i. Choose a type of option (call or put—it does not matter for this exercise).

        ii. For each volatility in the input matrix, find the Black-Scholes value of the corresponding option for the type you have chosen. For example, if you chose "call," then find the Black-Scholes price of a call option struck at 90 with four months to expiration.

        iii. Use the implied volatility tree to price the same option.

        iv. Record the answers in a table such as that shown in Table 3.

        v. Calculate the percentage error between the two answers.

        vi. Repeat the calculation for the other three options in the table.

    d. Repeat the same exercise, but this time build implied volatility trees of 25, 50, and 100 periods.

Discussion I

Consider the following questions for discussion.

    a. Why do implied volatility trees "perform" better on the input set of options as the number of periods grow?

    b. What sorts of errors on a tree account for this increased performance? (Hint: Think about stock price quantization errors.)

TABLE 3

Comparison of Black-Scholes Prices to Implied Volatility Tree Prices

Expiry	Strike	
4 months	/	/
8 months	/	/

c. As we use a greater number of periods, can we expect the tree to price options that are not part of the input set the same as Black-Scholes?

Discussion II

We now discuss some generalities concerning the preceding questions in discussion I. The mini smile in Table 2 represents the Black-Scholes implied volatilities for options in some hypothetical options market. The purpose of using implied volatility trees is to build a model that prices those options correctly. We see that low-period trees do not do an effective job in this regard. As the number of periods increases, however, we reduce the amount of stock price quantization error and begin to price the options closer to their "market" values.

The part C question is something of a red herring. The input set was not priced using Black-Scholes. Rather, the Black-Scholes formula was used for nothing more than converting prices to volatilities and back again. This is a common practice because it is a convenient way of comparing the prices at which the options trade.

5. The constant elasticity of variance model shows stock price movements and the relation to the volatility smile. Implied volatility trees provide an interesting way to study models that structure the volatility smile. In this exercise we look at the constant elasticity of variance (CEV) model, which posits that volatility, expressed as a function of time and spot price, has the following functional form:

$$\sigma(S, t) = \sigma_0 (S/S_0)^\beta \gamma(t) \tag{16}$$

$S_0 = $ today's spot price
$\sigma_0 = $ today's volatility
$\gamma = $ a function of time such that $\gamma(0) = 1$

The meaning of $\gamma(0) = 1$ is that today γ has a value of 1 so that $\sigma(S_0, 0) = \sigma_0$. For this reason, we call σ_0 today's volatility. The value σ_0 is also sometimes called the at-the-money volatility because if $S = S_0$, then $\sigma(S, t) = \sigma_0 \gamma(t)$.

We are going to examine the relationship between implied volatility (the volatility smile) and implied distributions.

The *Black-Scholes and Beyond Interactive Toolkit* Options Calculator allows you to enter a volatility smile whose functional form is the same as CEV. The specific form for the input volatility smile matrix is

$$\sigma(K, t) = \sigma_0 \cdot (K/S)^\beta (t + 1)^\alpha$$

where the user may enter σ_0, β, and α directly after depressing the FILL CEV button (see the beginning of this chapter for full details). The following exercises explore the implied distributions of CEV models.

a. Build an implied volatility tree using the CEV model with $\beta = -0.4, \alpha = 0$, and the other parameters set as follows:

$S = 100$
$T = 1$ year

$$r = 10\%$$
$$n = 20$$

To do this, use the CEV FILL button from the smile input matrix. Use a 5×5 input matrix. Note that the implied volatilities are the same for a given strike across all expirations (a consequence of $\alpha = 0$) and that implied volatility decreases as strike price increases.

b. Display the implied distribution of the tree.

c. Display the local volatility tree of the implied volatility tree.

d. Repeat the routine with $\beta = -0.6$, $\beta = -0.8$, and $\beta = -1.0$.[2] Note that making β more negative makes the "skew" of implied volatility steeper (you can see this by graphing the smile).

e. What happens to the local volatility structure of the tree as β becomes more negative?

f. What happens to the shape of the implied distribution as we make β more negative?

Discussion

Making β more negative has the effect of increasing implied volatility for low-strike options and increasing implied volatility for high-strike options. The same effect carries over to local volatilities. For a given time, as spot price decreases, local volatility increases; conversely, as spot price increases, local volatility decreases. This creates downward pressure on stock price movements: As stock prices drop, volatility increases, making large moves more likely. But the effect is not symmetric. If a large upward movement occurs, volatility again drops, decreasing the likelihood of more large movements. The overall effect is to trap the spot as it moves down by decreasing volatility if it tries to move back up.

6. This exercise examines the volatility smile and put-call parity. The volatility smile describes the "current" market for options. It says that relative to at-the-money options, out-of-the-money puts are expensive. Figure 3 displays a representative volatility smile of the S&P 500. Note that puts struck below 100% of the market have higher implied volatility than puts at-the-money. Does this mean that put call parity is violated?

Complete the following exercises:

a. Set the standard input parameters as follows:

$$S = \$100$$
$$T = 1 \text{ year}$$
$$r = 0\%$$
$$q = 0\%$$

b. Build a 30-period implied volatility tree with a 5×5 implied volatility smile matrix using the CEV FILL with coefficients $\alpha = 1.0$, $\beta = -0.6$, and $\sigma_0 = 18\%$.

c. Plot the smile. Note that out-of-the-money puts are indeed lower in price than at-the-money-puts.

---

[2] Warning: if β is set to a number 'too negative,' the skew becomes so steep that the implied volatility tree cannot be built.

FIGURE 3

The Volatility Smile for the S&P 500 Index for Two Different Expiration Dates

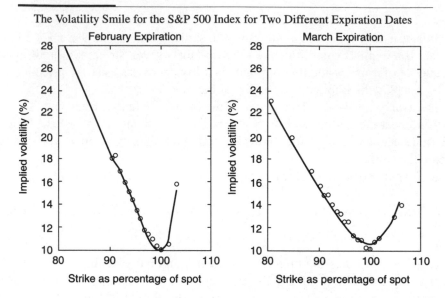

d. Compute the value of one-year vanilla put and call options struck at 90, 95, 100, and 105. Does put call parity hold for these options?

e. Why does put-call parity still hold even in the presence of the smile?

12

⑥ PRICING BARRIER OPTIONS

REVIEW OF CONCEPTS

Barrier options come in two flavors: knockout and knockin. Knockout options have a barrier price; this is a price that if reached, makes the contract null and void. Sometimes barrier options provide for a rebate or cash settlement paid to the long position should the option touch the barrier. Typically rebates are associated with knockout options, but, in principle, they can be used in any barrier option contract. Usually the rebate is some fraction of the option premium. Knockin options are exactly the opposite of knockout options: The barrier level for the option must be reached for the option to become active. Besides these features, barrier options have all the features of vanilla options: They can be European or American and come in put and call types.

This chapter deals exclusively with pricing barrier options on binomial trees, which is more complicated than pricing vanilla options because of the existence of the barrier. Moreover, there are certain issues dealing with price convergence that must be dealt with.

In-Out Parity

An important principle in pricing European barrier options is that of *in-out parity,* which simply states that the price of an *in* option plus the price of the corresponding out option (i.e., the out option with the same strike, expiration, and barrier) is equal to the price of the corresponding vanilla option. The in-out parity equation is written as

$$C_{in} + C_{out} = C_{vanilla}$$

Valuing Barrier Options

The main principle of pricing barrier options is the same for both knockin and knockout options. We view all barrier options as special cases of boundary value problems: At each point along the barrier, a target security must be paid to the long position should the spot price touch the barrier at

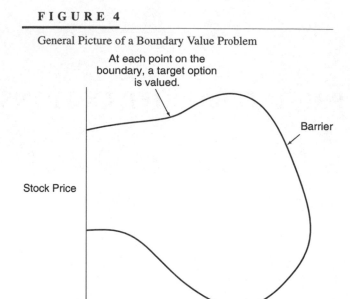

F I G U R E   4

General Picture of a Boundary Value Problem

that point (see Figure 4). Thus, when the barrier is touched, the option's life is over. If the option is a knockout, the rebate is paid, and the relationship between long and short position ends. If the option is a knockin, the short position hands over the vanilla option underlying the knockin option, and a distinct relationship between the long and short position begins. Thus, the short position's main worry is to be able to purchase the target option should the spot price touch the barrier.

In this sense, valuing barrier options is similar to valuing vanilla options on a tree. With vanilla options, we value the option at expiration [e.g., the value is $\max(S - K, 0)$ in the case of a call] and then work backward through the tree to value all nodes before expiration. That is, the short position must be prepared to pay the long position $S - K$ if the option expires in-the-money and nothing if the option expires out-of-the-money.

To value a barrier option, we first value every point along the barrier by valuing the corresponding target securities. Then we proceed by backward induction from the barrier. This procedure is summarized in Display 0.1.

Pitfalls

The main pitfall in pricing barrier options on binomial trees is that of convergence, which is the relationship between the real price of the option, assuming a continuous time stock process, and the discrete time price, based on pricing on a tree. Converge means that for any barrier option there is a tree with enough periods to produce a price as close as you want to the barrier option. The speed of convergence is a measure of how large the number of periods has to be. For example, if you want prices that are within $\frac{1}{100}$ of the continuous time price, do you need approximately 100 periods or 1,000 periods? The latter is obviously a case of slower convergence than the former.

The values of barrier options priced on trees converge more slowly than pricing vanilla options; moreover, the convergence pattern is saw toothed in nature. That is, as the number of periods increases, the prices do not move continuously closer to the continuous time value. Rather, there are setbacks along the way. This makes it difficult to gauge how good a barrier option price can be obtained on a binomial tree.

D I S P L A Y 0.1

How to Price Barrier Options

Pricing Barrier Options

To price barrier options on a binomial tree, we proceed in several steps. The following steps are illustrated in the accompanying diagram.

1. Build a binomial (stock) tree on which to price the option and define where the barrier is on the tree.
2. Find all the nodes along the barrier. These are the nodes that are touched immediately *after* first passage.
3. Value options at the nodes along the barrier according to the target option. If the option is a knockout option, the value of the target node is the cost of the rebate. If the option is a knockin option, then an option must be valued at each node along the barrier.
4. Use backward induction from the barrier. All nodes beyond the barrier (circled nodes in the figure) are to be ignored.

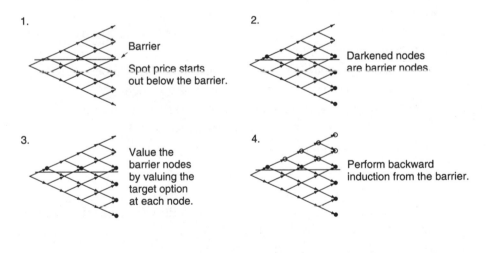

A very good way to improve the valuation procedure on a binomial tree is to use the Enhanced Numerical Method of Derman-Ergener-Kani. This method is explained in detail in *Black-Scholes and Beyond.* Given a binomial tree and a barrier option, the fundamental pricing difficulty is that the barrier may not be represented well by the tree. In fact, there are two barriers that appear on the tree: the effective barrier and the modified barrier. The effective barrier is the set of nodes immediately *after* the actual barrier on the tree, where "after" means after the spot price breaches the barrier (if the stock price starts above the barrier, "after" means below; if the stock price starts above the barrier, "after" means above). It is called the effective barrier because this is the barrier effectively used by the tree to price options. The other barrier, the modified barrier, is the set of nodes immediately before the actual barrier on the tree. The exercises at the end of the chapter illustrate its use.

COMPUTER TUTORIAL

To price barrier options on the *Black-Scholes and Beyond Interactive Toolkit* Options Calculator, you must use one of the tree methods. Analytic methods are not currently installed. You may choose between the regular pricing method and the enhanced binomial method of pricing, and you may set both the barrier and rebate levels.

Pricing Barrier Options

To price a barrier option using the *Black-Scholes and Beyond Interactive Toolkit* Options Calculator, proceed as follows:

1. Set the "Option Type menu" to one of
   a. Knockout call.
   b. Knockout put.
   c. Knockin call.
   d. Knockin put.

   A Barrier Level and Rebate slider display will appear.
2. Set the "Evaluation Method" menu to any of the tree methods: Cox-Ross-Rubinstein, Equal Probabilities, or Implied Volatility.
3. Set the "Underlying Type" menu to the desired underlying type.
4. Set the Stock Price slider display to the current stock price.
5. Set the Strike Price slider display to the strike price.
6. Set the Barrier Level slider display to the barrier level.
7. Set the Rebate slider display to the value of the rebate.
8. Set the Interest Rate slider display to the risk-free rate of interest.
9. Set the Divd Yield slider display to the dividend yield.
10. Set the Volatility slider display to the current volatility (if the evaluation method is implied volatility, you do not have to press this).
11. Set the Expiry slider display to the expiry.
12. (Optional) Enter a dividend schedule by pressing the ENTER DIV'DS button.
13. Select whether you want enhanced or not enhanced option pricing by pressing the ENHANCED/NOT ENHANCED button. This button toggles between displaying ENHANCED and NOT ENHANCED and prices accordingly.
14. Press EVALUATE OPTION.

The Options Calculator evaluates the option with the data you have given it. Once an option has been evaluated, you may display the various trees associated with the option.

Displaying the Option Pricing Trees

After you have priced a barrier option on a binomial tree, you may display any of the associated trees—stock price tree, European option price tree, American option price tree, transition probability tree, local volatility tree, or Arrow-Debreu price tree—by pulling down the "Display ..." menu to the desired tree type and then using the DISPLAY ... button.

A useful feature of the tree display function is that the effective barrier is highlighted on all tree displays associated with a barrier option.

- **All trees.** You may select the number of digits of precision for the output of the tree by selecting Output Precision (trees) in the "Configuration" menu in the main option pricing screen. This affects the maximum number of periods the tree will display. If the tree has more than 12 periods (for two-digit precision) more than 11 periods (four-digit precision) or 9 periods (six-digit precision), only the first 12, 11, or 9 periods are displayed, respectively.
- **Stock price tree.** Set the "Display ..." to Stock Price, and press the DISPLAY button. The stock price tree used to price your option will appear. When the tree is displayed, the barrier nodes are highlighted. This means each node directly after the barrier will display its value in a color different than in the rest of the nodes.
- **European option tree.** Set the "Display ..." menu to Euro Options, and press the DISPLAY button.

QUESTIONS FOR BASIC UNDERSTANDING

1. Set the Options Calculator to the following parameter values:

$$S = \$100 \text{ (stock price)}$$
$$K = \$100 \text{ (strike price)}$$
$$B = \$110 \text{ (barrier level)}$$
$$R = \$0 \text{ (rebate)}$$
$$T = 1 \text{ year}$$
$$\sigma = 15\% \text{ (volatility)}$$
$$r = 10\% \text{ (risk-free rate)}$$
$$q = 0\% \text{ (dividend yield)}$$
$$n = 25 \text{ (number of periods)}$$

Complete the following set of exercises:

a. Price a European knockout call with these parameters.
b. Price a European knockin call with these parameters.

    c. Does in-out parity hold?

    d. Now repeat the parts a, b, and c, but evaluate the options with 50 and then 75 periods. In-out parity should hold more precisely. Why?

Discussion

The answer to this question is actually difficult to see without knowing one vital piece of information: the Options Calculator price target options (options along the barrier) using Black-Scholes. As the tree itself is a binomial tree, in-out parity would only hold exactly if the options along the barrier were priced using a tree. Why is this the case?

    As we increase the number of periods in the stock price tree, the vanilla option prices converge to Black-Scholes, and therefore in-out parity holds more precisely.

    2. This set of exercises examines the difference in values between European and American barrier options. Use the following set of parameters:

$$S = \$100 \text{ (stock price)}$$
$$K = \$100 \text{ (strike price)}$$
$$B = \$110 \text{ (barrier level)}$$
$$R = \$0 \text{ (rebate)}$$
$$T = 1 \text{ year}$$
$$\sigma = 10\% \text{ (volatility)}$$
$$r = 10\% \text{ (risk-free rate)}$$
$$q = 0\% \text{ (dividend yield)}$$
$$n = 10 \text{ (number of periods)}$$

Use the same set of input parameters as the previous set of exercises, set the number of periods to at least 25.

    a. Value a European and an American knockout call option with these parameters. There should be a large price difference (depending on how many periods you use). What is the intuitive explanation for this difference?

    b. Now display both the European and American option pricing trees simultaneously. The effective barrier nodes (the nodes immediately above the barrier) will be highlighted on both trees, and the American early exercise nodes will be marked with a "sliver" on their right side in the American option tree. Note the nodes directly below the barrier node at time 0.90 for both trees. What is significant about the price differences?

    c. Compute the option delta at node (9,6) for both the European and American options. [Node (9,6) is the node directly below the barrier at time 0.90.] What is significant about the deltas?

Discussion

Many of the nodes along the barrier are American early exercise nodes. The interesting point is that the intrinsic values are often much greater than the holding values of the options at these nodes. This is due to the extreme effect of the barrier. For example, at node (9,6) the American option has a delta of approximately -1.38. In practical terms, if the stock price moves up, the option will knock out. Consequently, the holder of the long will position will exercise at this point.

3. Now complete the same exercises as in question 2, but with a knockin call option.

     a. Why are all the nodes below node (10,7) in both the European and American option tree equal to zero?

Discussion I

Node (10,7) is the barrier node, and no node below it can be reached by a node that has touched the barrier. As such, if the option reaches any of the nodes below (10,7) it will not have knocked in and will expire worthless (despite the fact that the corresponding vanilla option is in the money).

Using the same knockin option as in part a, complete the following exercises:

     b. What is the target option at node (9,7)?

     c. Price the target option at node (9,7) using the Black-Scholes formula (use the Options Calculator), and confirm that it has been priced correctly. (Hint: What risk-free rate of interest and volatility do you use?)

Discussion II

The target option at node (9,7) is a European call option struck at $100, expiring at time 1.0. The stock value at node (9,7) is $117.1300. To value the option we need a risk-free rate and a volatility to input into the Black-Scholes formula. Since we are using a Cox-Ross-Rubinstein tree, volatility and risk-free rate are the same at every node; therefore, we use a volatility of 10% and a risk-free rate of 10% to value the option.[1]

Therefore, to value the target option we need to value (using Black-Scholes) a vanilla call option struck at $100, expiring in 0.1 year (expiry time is 1.0 year, current time is 0.9) with current stock price equal to $117.1300. Doing this computation using the Options Calculator yields $18.1250, which is exactly the number displayed in the European option tree.

4. This exercise examines the effect of higher volatility. Suppose the node volatility at node (9,7) were significantly greater than 10%. This could be the case if, for example, there were a positive correlation between stock price and volatility. Would this significantly affect the value of the option? Repeat the same question but with a barrier of $97.

Discussion

When the strike is $100 and the barrier is $110, the target option is deep in-the-money. As a consequence, the vega of the target option is very low, and high volatility does not significantly affect the target option value; therefore, it does not significantly affect the knockin option price.

---

[1] Actually, the Options Calculator values the option by computing the local volatility at the barrier node and uses that volatility as the input to the tree. For low-period Cox-Ross-Rubinstein trees, this volatility is slightly different than the input volatility and, therefore, creates small errors in valuation.

On the other hand, with a $97 barrier, the option knocks in with significant vega, and an increase in volatility would increase option price significantly. (For more on this, see Chapter 13.)

5. This exercise examines the effect of a rebate. Set the input parameters as follows:

$$S = \$100 \text{ (stock price)}$$
$$K = \$100 \text{ (strike price)}$$
$$B = \$110 \text{ (barrier level)}$$
$$R = \$1 \text{ (rebate)}$$
$$T = 1 \text{ year}$$
$$\sigma = 10\% \text{ (volatility)}$$
$$r = 10\% \text{ (risk-free rate)}$$
$$q = 0\% \text{ (dividend yield)}$$
$$n = 10 \text{ (number of periods)}$$

Complete the following exercises:

a. By how much did the option value increase by raising the rebate from $0 to $1?

b. Increase the value of the rebate from $1 to $2. What happens to the price of the European knockout option? What happens to the price of the corresponding American option? What explains this difference? To answer this question, view the European and American option pricing trees.

Discussion

Increasing the rebate has the following effect in general: If there are stock price paths that pay off at the barrier, they will pay off a greater amount. Put another way, the rebate places a value on each barrier node. If the spot price path touches one of the barrier nodes, the payoff is triggered. Therefore, increasing the rebate will increase option value unless the barrier nodes are never reached. Since the American option value does not increase upon increasing the rebate, we conclude that those nodes are never reached. In other words, the option is always exercised prior to reaching the barrier. Examine the American Option tree to confirm this.

6. A client would like to purchase the following option contract from your firm. They would like to buy a put option on the S&P 500 struck 10% below the market with the following specification addition to the standard contract:

The client will only pay the premium if the option goes in-the-money.

a. What premium should you charge should the index level reach 10%? How can you use barrier options to price this deal?

Discussion I

The put option starts out-of-the-money, and the client only wants to pay for the put protection if the stock price drops 10%. To make this concrete, let's set up the following scenario:

$$S = \$100 \text{ (stock price)}$$
$$K = \$90 \text{ (strike price)}$$
$$T = 1 \text{ year}$$

$r = 10\%$ (risk-free rate)
$q = 0\%$ (dividend yield)
$\sigma = 10\%$ (volatility)

Essentially the client only wants to be short the 90-put if the index drops to 90. Therefore, they want some sort of knockin put option with a barrier level of $90. But they want to pay you a premium if the option knocks in. Therefore, they are buying a knockin put with a negative rebate (they pay you). The last thing to determine is the value of the rebate. This value is determined by the one remaining piece of data about the option: the client does not want to pay an up-front premium. Therefore, the correct rebate is the one in which the current option premium is zero.

      b. Use the Options Calculator to compute the negative rebate (you will have to iteratively search for the correct value). How does it compare with the value of the vanilla option?

Discussion II
The vanilla put is significantly cheaper than the more complicated security. The put can be regarded as an insurance policy against market drops greater than 10%. The put option is deep out-of-the-money, so its premium is low. However, it is also very unlikely that the underlying price will ever reach $90. If it does, however, the option will be in-the-money at that point and have significant value. Thus, the long position pays a much larger premium at that point.

      In general, the rebate property of barrier options can be used to price a variety of options having a "pay later" feature. That is, any option whose premium is delayed until the spot price reaches a certain level can be valued as described by using a barrier option with a negative rebate

      7. This exercise will walk you through the details of the enhanced numerical method for pricing barrier options for knockout calls. In a subsequent problem we will examine in detail the effect of the enhanced method. Set the Options Calculator as follows:

    i. Set the input parameters as follows:

$S = \$100$ (stock price)
$K = \$100$ (strike price)
$B = \$110$ (barrier level)
$R = \$0$ (rebate)
$T = 1$ year
$\sigma = 10\%$ (volatility)
$r = 10\%$ (risk-free rate)
$q = 0\%$ (dividend yield)
$n = 5$ (number of periods)

   ii. Set the "Option Type" menu to Knockout Call.
  iii. Set the method to Not Enhanced.
   iv. Press the EVALUATE OPTION button.
    v. Display the European Option tree.
   vi. Repeat the foregoing procedure with the method set to Enhanced.
  vii. Display the stock price tree.

We are going to work through the computation of the barrier node values for the enhanced tree. First let's recall a definition: The barrier nodes of the stock price tree are the nodes directly beyond the barrier. These nodes are highlighted on the stock and option price trees you have displayed.

The effective barrier is the barrier the tree actually uses to price the option. In the current example, the effective barrier consists of the first nodes at each time step that lie above $110. At time $t = 0.60$, the effective barrier is $114.36; at time $t = 0.80$, the effective barrier is $119.59; at time $t = 1.00$, the effective barrier is $114.36.

The modified barrier consists of the nodes directly below the effective barrier. Here is a table of modified barrier nodes:

Time Step	Modified Barrier Node Value
$t = 0.60$	$104.57
$t = 0.80$	109.36
$t = 1.00$	104.57

The goal of the enhanced method is to compute the node values directly before (below in this case) the barrier two ways: first assuming the barrier is the effective barrier and then assuming the barrier is the modified barrier. These values are then interpolated according to the relative distances of the effective and modified barriers to the actual barrier.

For the nodes at time $t = 0.80$, complete the following exercises (refer to *Black-Scholes and Beyond,* Chapter 11 for the formulaic details):

a. Compute the value of the node in the European option tree directly below the barrier at time $t = 0.80$, assuming the barrier is the effective barrier. This is the effective barrier value of the modified barrier node, V_e in the notation of *Black-Scholes and Beyond.* (Answer: $V_e = \$1.28$)

b. Compute the value of the node in the European option tree directly below the barrier at time $t = 0.80$, assuming the barrier is the modified barrier. This is the modified barrier value of the modified barrier node, V_m in the notation of *Black-Scholes and Beyond.* (Answer: $V_m = \$0.00$)

c. What is the price difference between the effective barrier and the actual barrier at time $t = 0.80$? (Answer: $B_e - B_a = \$9.59$)

d. What is the price difference between the modified barrier and the actual barrier at time $t = 0.80$? (Answer: $B_a - B_m = \$0.64$)

e. What is the price difference between the effective and modified barrier at time $t = 0.80$? (Answer: $B_e - B_m = \$10.28$)

f. What is the interpolated value of the node in the European option tree directly below the barrier? Here is the formula from Eq. (11.5.1) in *Black-Scholes and Beyond:*

$$V = \frac{B_a - B_m}{B_e - B_m} V_e + \frac{B_e - B_a}{B_e - B_m} V_m$$

[Answer: $(0.64/10.28) \cdot 1.28 + (9.59/10.28) \cdot 0.00 = 0.08$]

Discussion

The unenhanced node value is $1.28, while the enhanced node value is only $0.08. This reflects the fact that the effective barrier ($119.59) is quite far from the actual barrier. Moving the barrier down one notch on the tree turns node (4,3) into a barrier node (for the modified barrier). In this guise it has zero value. However, node (4,3) is very close to the barrier since its value is $109.36. Therefore, the value of zero dominates the overvalue of node (4,3), which is why the enhanced value is so much smaller than the unenhanced value.

Now repeat the preceding calculations for node (3,2).

8. In this exercise we will concentrate on the enhanced numerical method for a knockin put option. Set the Options Calculator parameters as follows:

i. Set the input parameters

$$S = \$100 \text{ (stock price)}$$
$$K = \$100 \text{ (strike price)}$$
$$B = \$90 \text{ (barrier level)}$$
$$R = \$0 \text{ (rebate)}$$
$$T = 1 \text{ year}$$
$$\sigma = 10\% \text{ (volatility)}$$
$$r = 10\% \text{ (risk-free rate)}$$
$$q = 0\% \text{ (dividend yield)}$$
$$n = 5 \text{ (number of periods)}$$

ii. Set the "Option Type" menu to Knockin Put.

iii. Set the method to Not Enhanced.

iv. Press the EVALUATE OPTION button.

v. Display the European option tree.

vi. Display the stock price tree.

vii. Repeat this procedure with the method set to Enhanced.

Now complete the following set of exercises:

a. What is the actual barrier for this option?

b. What is the effective barrier for this option?

c. What is the modified barrier?

Discussion I

This option is a down-and-in put option. The actual barrier is $90. The effective barrier is the set of nodes just beyond the barrier at each time step. At time steps $t = 0.00, t = 0.20$, and $t = 0.40$, there is no effective barrier because all of the nodes are above the actual barrier. That is, there is no node just below the barrier. At time step $t = 0.60$, the effective barrier is $87.44; at time step $t = 0.80$, the effective barrier is $83.62 and at time $t = 1.00$, the effective barrier is $87.44.

The modified barrier is the set of nodes just above the actual barrier. Here is a complete list of where the barriers are:

Time Step	Effective Barrier	Modified Barrier
$t = 0.00$	N/A	$100.00
$t = 0.20$	N/A	95.63
$t = 0.40$	N/A	91.44
$t = 0.60$	$87.44	95.63
$t = 0.80$	83.62	91.44
$t = 1.00$	87.44	95.63

Now continue with the next set of questions:

a. Display the European option price tree for the preceding option.

b. Value the effective barrier nodes of the unenhanced European option tree.

Discussion II

The nodes along the barrier are valued according to the target option, a vanilla put. To value these options, consider the following chart of the effective barrier nodes and target options:

Time Step	Stock Price	Target Option
$t = 1.00$	$87.44	P(100,1.00)
$t = 0.80$	83.62	P(100,1.00)
$t = 0.60$	87.44	P(100,1.00)

The effective barrier nodes at all three time steps represent a vanilla put option struck at 100 expiring at time 1.00. The first option has expired, so its value is $S - K = \$100 - \$87.44 = \$12.56$.

The second option has 0.20 year to expiration; value the put using a volatility of 10% and a risk-free rate of 10%.

The third option has 0.40 year to expiration. Do the following:

a. Use the Options Calculator to value a vanilla put struck at 100, when the strike price is at $87.45 and the time to expiration is 0.40 year. Set the risk-free rate to 10%, and the volatility to 10%.

b. Compare the answer you got earlier to the value of the effective barrier node at time 0.60 of the European option tree.

c. The option values should be slightly different. What is the cause of this?

Discussion III

To resolve the issue, display the local volatility tree. Note that the local volatility at each node is approximately 9%, instead of the 10% input volatility. This is a result of stock price quantization error on a tree. The valuation method we use takes as an input volatility to the target options along the barrier the local volatility of the barrier nodes.

To continue with the enhanced method calculation, do the following exercises:

    a. Revalue the same option using the enhanced method.

    b. Value the modified barrier nodes.

Discussion IV

The modified barrier is the set of nodes directly above the actual barrier. We will explain the valuation of the target option at each time on the tree; in all cases we have to remember to use an input volatility of 9% (round the local volatility for convenience).

    At time $t = 1.00$, the modified barrier is node (5,3) and has a stock value of $95.63; the option has expired at this time and is therefore worth $4.37.

    At time $t = 0.80$, the modified barrier is node (4,2) and has a stock value of $91.44. To value this node we use Black-Scholes to value a vanilla put on a stock worth $91.44, with input volatility 9%, a risk-free rate of 10%, and 0.20 year to expiration. This value is $6.6450. Note this is *not* the value you will see in the European option tree for the enhanced method. That value is the value arrived at by interpolating the effective value and the modified value.

Now complete the enhanced numerical method calculation by computing the enhanced values of the modified barrier nodes:

    a. Value the option using the unenhanced method.

    b. Display the European option tree.

    c. What are the modified barrier nodes for this tree? Fill in the following table.

Time	Modified Node Option Value
$t = 1.00$	
$t = 0.80$	
$t = 0.60$	
$t = 0.40$	
$t = 0.20$	
$t = 0.00$	

    d. Why is node (5,2) equal to zero?

    e. Now compute the enhanced values by interpolation at each node.

    9. *Black-Scholes and Beyond* discussed the convergence properties of pricing barrier options on a binomial tree. In this exercise we explore when it is the most beneficial to use the enhanced method.

a. Set the input parameters as follows:

$$S = \$100 \text{ (stock price)}$$
$$K = \$100 \text{ (strike price)}$$

$$R = \$0 \text{ (rebate)}$$
$$T = 1 \text{ year}$$
$$B = \$90$$
$$\sigma = 10\% \text{ (volatility)}$$
$$r = 10\% \text{ (risk-free rate)}$$
$$q = 0\% \text{ (dividend yield)}$$

b. Make a graph of number of periods in a binomial tree versus option value for a European knockout call. Use the unenhanced method. Would you expect the convergence properties of the corresponding knockin call to be any better? Why?

c. Replot the graph using the enhanced method. Does it improve the convergence properties?

d. The enhanced method takes significantly longer to compute a given number of periods than the corresponding unenhanced method for the same option. Explain this. Is the extra computation time justified?

10. This exercise provides an example where the binomial tree performs particularly badly on a down-and-out call option, thereby showing very bad convergence. Set the input parameters as follows:

$$S = \$95$$
$$K = \$100$$
$$B = \$90$$
$$T = 1 \text{ year}$$
$$\sigma = 25\%$$
$$r = 10\%$$
$$q = 0\%$$

The value of a knockout call option with these specifications is $6.00, and the delta is 1.12 when valued using an analytic formula. This set of exercises explores how well a constant volatility tree performs in converging to this value. Complete the following:

a. Value the knockout call option on a 50-period Cox-Ross-Rubinstein tree.

b. Value the knockout call option on a 300-period tree (some machines may not have enough memory for this; if so, use 200 periods). The value is still not particularly close to the barrier option value. Let's explore why:
   i. Display the stock price tree and the European option pricing tree.
   ii. What is the distance from the actual barrier to the effective barrier? (The effective barrier will be highlighted.)
   iii. How does this distance affect the valuation procedure?
   iv. What general principles can you draw from this regarding the valuation of long-term options on high-volatility stocks?

Discussion

To increase your intuition in the area of pricing barrier options on binomial trees, consider Table 4, which lists the analytic prices for barrier options.

TABLE 4

Analytic Values for Barrier Options
with Current Stock Price = $95, Strike
Price = $100, Barrier = $90; risk-free
rate = 10%, and dividend yield = 0%.

		Volatility	
Expiration	10%	15%	25%
2 weeks	0.0049	0.0644	0.4217
2 months	0.4354	1.0433	2.1796
6 months	2.5614	3.4723	4.3294
1 year	5.8510	6.1008	5.9970
2 years	11.7053	9.9902	8.0522

    a. Value the options with two weeks to expiration on a Cox-Ross-Rubinstein binomial tree. Answer the following questions:

        i. What is (roughly) the minimum number of periods necessary to accurately price the options within 10% of their analytic values[2]? What about within 5%?

        ii. Which option volatility is easiest to calculate (for the two-week expiry option) on a tree? Why? To aid your intuition, display the stock price tree for each level of volatility, and find out where the effective barrier is.

        iii. For a 50-period Cox-Ross-Rubinstein tree, what percentage of the analytic value is the tree value?

    b. Repeat exercise a with the two-month, six-month, one-year, and two-year options.

    c. Based on your findings, list some general guidelines for when it is "safe" to value barrier options on a binomial tree and when other methods should be sought.

    11. This set of exercises looks into the question of the delta of a barrier option near the barrier.

Barrier option deltas in dramatic ways compared to their vanilla cousins, due to the singularity of the price behavior at or near the barrier. To gain a better understanding of the phenomenon, we will make some graphs of the delta of a barrier option. Complete the following set of exercises.

    a. Set the input parameters as follows:

$$S = \$100$$
$$K = \$90$$
$$\sigma = 15\%$$
$$r = 10\%$$
$$q = 0\%$$
$$T = 30 \text{ days}$$
$$n = 20$$

---

[2]That is, if V_a is the analytic value and V_t is the tree value, how many periods are necessary to have $V_t/V_a > 0.90$?

Now set the following graph menus:

- Option type: Knockout call.
- Evaluation method: Binomial C-R-R.
- Z-axis: Option delta.
- X-axis: Barrier.

Click on the *Plot X-Z* button, and wait for the graph to appear. Answer the following questions:

i. At what barrier level is the option delta the greatest?
ii. At what barrier level is the option delta the least?
iii. What are the largest and smallest values of the delta?

b. Redo the above exercise, but this time set the volatility parameter to 30 percent. Before displaying the graph, try to determine the answer to the following questions.

i. Will the largest and smallest values of the delta increase or decrease?
ii. What is the intuitive explanation for this answer?

Now redo this exercise, but lower the volatility to 5 percent.

Discussion

Increasing the volatility actually decreases the size of the barrier. This is to some extent opposite to one's immediate assessment of the situation because typically the underlying's volatility augments everything to do with an option. In the case of a knockout option's delta, however, the tables are turned and increase volatility actually decreases the delta near the barrier. The reason is the asymmetric nature of knocking out. Knocking out causes a sudden drop to nothing in option value. The less volatile the stock is, the more dramatic this reduction in value. Why? We develop this idea more fully in the next exercise.

12. This set of exercises tries to delve into the question, why does the delta of a knockout call option decrease near the barrier when volatility decreases.

a. Value a knockout call option using a 30-period binomial tree and the following set of input parameters:

$$S = \$100$$
$$K = \$98$$
$$B = \$98 \text{ (the barrier value dddd)}$$
$$R = \$0 \text{ (the rebate)}$$
$$\sigma = 10\%$$
$$r = 10\%$$
$$q = 0\%$$
$$T = 30 \text{ days}$$

b. Display the European option price tree by i) setting the *Display... tree* menu to *Euro Option* and ii) clicking the *Display... tree* button. Next display the stock price tree. Leave the displays up.

c. Value a second knockout call option with the same parameters but with a volatility of 15 percent. Display the European option tree and stock price tree for this option. Now answer the following questions:

- When the stock price is near the barrier level, what, in general, does an increase volatility do to the value of the option? Why? (Hint: Does increasing volatility increase or decrease the probability of knocking out in this case?)
- Suppose we have a stock that is extremely volatile, and its price is only slightly above a barrier level of $100, and suppose there is a knockout call option with strike of $100.50 and barrier of $100. If the price moves down, the option knocks out and is worthless. If the price moves up, the option moves into the money and becomes valuable. What is the relationship in this case between stock price and option delta? Verify your answer by making a graph.

13

⑥ PRICING BARRIER OPTIONS IN THE PRESENCE OF THE SMILE

This chapter moves beyond *Black-Scholes and Beyond* and provides an in-depth look at the relationship between the volatility smile and barrier options. In *Black-Scholes and Beyond,* we emphasized two points regarding the volatility smile and barrier options:

- Barrier options are more sensitive to the overall structure of stock price volatility than vanilla options.
- Barrier options can be priced "in the presence of the smile" using Implied Volatility trees.

One thing *Black-Scholes and Beyond* did not do was analyze the effect of the volatility structure on the pricing of barrier options. In particular we are interested in knowing to how great a degree the volatility smile affects the pricing of barrier options. To aid our study, we will use the CEV model (provided in the Options Calculator, see Chapter 11) and the Implied Volatility trees model of stock price movements. The computer tutorials for this can be found in Chapter 11.

ANALYSIS: BARRIER OPTIONS IN A NEGATIVE SKEW

The analysis we will perform demonstrates the effect of a negative volatility skew on a variety of barrier options. First set the standard input parameters as follows:

$S = \$100$
$K = \$100$
$T = 6$ months
$r = 10\%$
$q = 0\%$
$n = 25$ periods

TABLE 5

Option Prices and Deltas for Knockout Call Options with a Variety of Different Scenarios

	Barrier		
	90	**95**	**105**
CRR (15%) : price/delta			
$\beta = -0.3$: price/delta	$6.93/0.72		
$\beta = -0.6$: price/delta			
$\beta = -0.9$: price/delta			

Your task will be to fill in Table 5, using the Options Calculator and then complete a set of exercises. Let's discuss the contents of Table 5. Each cell of the table should contain the value and delta of a certain knockout call option under certain market conditions. The market conditions are controlled by the CEV coefficient β. Recall that the more negative the coefficient β is, the more skewed the implied stock price distribution is toward negative returns. The general trend is that if stock price increases, then volatility decreases; conversely, the more stock price decreases, the more volatility increases.

One of the cells of the table is already filled in. Here is how the values for that node were computed:

1. Build a 5×5 smile with the CEV FILL feature of the smile input matrix, using the values $\alpha = 0, \beta = -0.3, \sigma_0 = 15\%$.
2. Build the 25-period implied volatility tree.
3. Value a knockout call option with barrier level-$90, and input parameters set as indicated. Record the option value and delta.

To fill in the row labeled CRR (15%), value the various knockout call options on a 25-period Cox-Ross-Rubinstein tree with an input volatility of 15%. That is, we will be comparing the value of options in a constant 15% volatility world to option values in a world with at-the-money volatility of 15% but with spot price dependence governed by the CEV model.

Now answer the following questions for each of the three barrier options studied in Table 5:

1. What is the relationship between the CRR price of the option and the "skew" price?
2. As the CEV coefficient gets more negative, what is the general trend in prices for the $90 barrier call options as compared with the Cox-Ross-Rubinstein prices?
3. Suppose we sell a $90 (respectively $95, $105) barrier European knockout call to a client and value the option using a constant volatility model. If, in reality, the stock price movements give a CEV smile, what will the effect be on delta hedging?

Now repeat these exercise for knockin options as well as for options of different expirations. Complete the following exercises setting the input parameters as follows:

$S = \$100$
$K = \$100$
$B = \$95$ (*Barrier*)
$R = \$0$ Rebate
$\sigma = 15\%$
$r = 10\%$
$q = 0\%$
$T = 1$ year

Build a 40-period implied volatility tree with the CEV model using the following input parameters:

$\alpha = 0$
$\beta = -0.3$
$\sigma = 15\%$

Note: For best performance, use a volatility input matrix of at least three strikes and three expiries.
Now do the following:

- Evaluate a knockout call option with the following input parameters

  $K = \$100$
  $B = \$95$ (*Barrier*)
  $R = \$0$ Rebate

- Display the local volatility tree
- Display the European option pricing tree.

Answer the following questions:

- What are the values of volatility near the barrier of the option, and how do these volatilities compare with the present at-the-money volatility (i.e., the base volatility of the CEV model, σ_0)?
- How do you think these values affect the value of the knockout option?
- Do the local volatilities of the stock price nodes near the barrier affect the knockout options price, considering that the value of the option is always zero at the barrier? (Hint: consider in-out parity, see *Black-Scholes and Beyond*, pp. 436–38).

14

STUDYING OPTIONS THROUGH SIMULATED HEDGING

THE HEDGING GAME

To better understand Black-Scholes hedging we have provided **SimuHedge** as a tool to simulate the actual Black-Scholes hedging of an option. This game will take us beyond what was learned about hedging in *Black-Scholes and Beyond* by introducing the notion of a rebalancing strategy. The following is a description of the hedging game and a small tutorial. In the rest of the chapter, you will be asked a variety of questions about hedging, all of which can be answered by playing the hedging game using SimuHedge.

Here is how the game works. You will be hedging a vanilla European call option that you have written for a client. The client and your firm have agreed to a certain price for the option; your goal is to hedge the option to a profit. You will hedge the option through buying the underlying and selling a bond to raise cash. As the game progresses, you will rebalance the hedge at certain intervals; your goal is to make money by replicating the payoff of the option.

1. Specify the following Black-Scholes parameters: stock price, strike price, risk-free interest rate, volatility of underlying, and time to expiration.

2. Select from one of the following stock process options: constant known volatility, constant unknown volatility, stochastic volatility, or stock price jump. Here is a more detailed description of each:

a. With the constant known volatility you specify the option's volatility, and then a "perfect" geometric Brownian motion is generated with that volatility. All of your hedge parameters are automatically computed with the same volatility.

b. With the constant unknown volatility, the volatility is constant, but you do not know it! Rather, you are told approximately what the volatility is, but you do not know how accurate the approximation is.

    c. With the stochastic volatility options, a mean reverting stochastic volatility stock process is generated (see *Black-Scholes and Beyond,* p. 356). You are asked to specify the parameters of the process (mean reversion strength, etc.).

    d. With the stock price jump options, random stock price jumps are introduced into the stock process. You are asked to specify a certain "jump size," which tells how big the jumps will be when compared with the stock price, and "jump frequency," which tells how often the jumps occur.

    3. Choose an interest rate environment from one of the following: constant interest rates or random (stochastic) mean reverting interest rates.

    4. Select a rebalancing strategy: constant rehedge period, delta tolerance strategy, or stock tolerance strategy. Here is a more detailed description of each strategy:

    a. The constant rehedge period is similar to what was displayed in *Black-Scholes and Beyond,* pp. 208–17. You choose an amount of time (e.g., two days) and then rebalance the Black-Scholes hedge once every two weeks for the remainder of the option's life.

    b. The delta tolerance strategy prompts you to rehedge each time the delta of the underlying moves beyond a certain "tolerance" from its last position. For example, if the last time the delta was computed, it was at 0.8, and you choose a tolerance of 0.05, then you will not be prompted to rehedge until the delta dips below 0.75 or above 0.85.

    c. The stock tolerance strategy is similar to the delta tolerance strategy except the tolerance is on the stock price and not the delta. Thus, you are prompted to rebalance the Black-Scholes hedge whenever the stock price moves beyond a certain tolerance of the stock price the last time the hedge was rebalanced.

    5. Rebalance your portfolio by choosing an amount of stock to purchase. The SimuHedge game automatically sets the rebalancing based on the historical volatility.

    6. Finally, hedge. As the option's life evolves, you will watch several screens that display your Black-Scholes option value as well as your hedge parameter values and your profit and loss.

REVIEW OF CONCEPTS

In this chapter we will use the hedging game to set up and hedge a vanilla European call option in the simplest possible trading scenario:

- The stock follows a perfect geometric Brownian motion.
- Interest rates are constant.

You will play the game to help answer the questions at the end of the chapter. We now review some of the basic concepts of hedging.

    In Black-Scholes hedging, the costs of hedging are divided into two different categories: setup costs and rebalancing costs. Setup costs are all of the costs incurred in "putting on" the hedge, while rebalancing costs are all of the costs incurred in rebalancing the hedge.

    The Black-Scholes hedging strategy for a short vanilla European call option requires the hedger to hold Δ shares of the option long and short a bond. The amount of the bond is taken from the Black-Scholes formula:

$$C = N(d_1)Se^{-q(T-t)} - e^{-r(T-t)}N(d_2)K$$

where

$$d_1 = \frac{\log(S/K) + (r - q + \sigma^2/2)(T - t)}{\sigma\sqrt{T - t}}$$

$$d_2 = d_1 - \sigma\sqrt{T - t}$$

S = stock price

K = strike price

r = risk-free rate of interest (per annum)

σ = volatility of the stock (per annum)

$T - t$ = time until expiration (in years)

q = continuous dividend yield (per annum)

The hedging strategy requires that you hold $N(d_1)$ shares long and short a bond expiring at expiration to $N(d_2)K$. In theory, if the stock follows a geometric Brownian motion (see *Black-Scholes and Beyond,* Chapter 3) with known volatility σ, if risk-free rates are a constant value r, if the hedger continuously rebalances the option, and if $N(d_1)$ and $N(d_2)$ are computed with the correct values of r and σ, then the strategy will be self-financing and replicating. The exercises at the end of the chapter help show you what happens when hedging does not go exactly as planned.

COMPUTER TUTORIAL

There are several screens associated with the SimuHedge game.

- The SimuHedge Setup Screen is designed for choosing the stock price environment and option you will hedge.
- The SimuHedge Main Screen is the main screen in which you hedge options. You calculate your rebalancing, and then you see the stock price evolve, check your hedge parameters, and choose your hedging strategy.
- The SimuHedge Summary Screen appears when you have completed hedging your option. It displays a summary of hedging costs, volatility, and stock price movement.

To play the game you first must set up the game.

The Setup Screen

The SimuHedge Setup screen is divided into several parts as discussed here.

1. Basic Stock Features refer to the stock price (and more general economic) properties of the Black-Scholes world:

    a. Stock price.

    b. Stock volatility.

    c. Risk-free interest rate.

    d. Dividend yield.

Unless you direct SimuHedge otherwise, all of these parameters are set to be constant throughout the life of the option. You may adjust the parameter values by sliding the sliders or typing directly into the display boxes.

    2. Option Properties include the following list:

        a. Strike price.

        b. Expiry.

        c. Stock lot size (choose between 1 and 100 shares).

        d. Size of option (100, 1,000, or 10,000 shares).

The stock lot size is not really an option property. It is the minimum number of shares of stock you can buy or sell at a time. The expiry is always measured in days, and the option may be written on 100, 1,000, or 10,000 shares.

    3. Advanced Stock Features allow you to deviate your trading world from the Black-Scholes world. The default values of the advanced stock features are set so that

        a. Volatility is constant.

        b. Interest rates are constant.

        c. The stock price never jumps.

        d. Markets are 100% liquid; there is no bid-ask spread.

You may adjust any of the parameters in the Advanced Features section to move away from these assumptions. Here is a description of each of the features.

- *Vol of Vol* allows the introduction of stochastic volatility into stock price movements. The higher the stochasticity of volatility, the more wildly volatility will fluctuate. Default value = 0.

- *Correlation* measures the correlation between stock price and volatility. This correlation ranges from −1 (100% negative correlation between stock price and volatility) and 1 (100% correlation between stock price and volatility). A correlation of 0 means stock price and volatility are uncorrelated. See *Black-Scholes and Beyond,* pp. 349–50 for more on this. Default value = 0.

- *Vol of Risk-Free* measures the volatility of risk-free rates. If you set this to something greater than zero, the risk-free rate is set off on a geometric Brownian motion of its own, and this parameter controls the volatility of interest rate movements. Default value = 0.

- *Reversion Strength* allows you to introduce mean reversion into the stock price volatility model. The greater the reversion strength, the more powerful the pull of the volatility back to the mean volatility. For more on this, see *Black-Scholes and Beyond,* pp. 346–47. Default value = 0.

- *Mean Vol* is the mean volatility that the volatility reverts to in case there is a positive reversion strength. If the reversion strength is set to zero, then the mean volatility has no effect on volatility changes. Default value = 0.

- *Rate Drift* is the size of the drift of the geometric Brownian motion for interest rates. Default value = 0.

- *Liquidity* controls the size of the bid-ask spread. A liquidity of 100 means 100% liquidity 100% of the time. As liquidity drops from 100, the bid-ask spread increases, increasing trading costs when you hedge. Default value = 100.

- *Jump Frequency* controls the frequency of jumps in the market. The value in the box tells you the average number of jumps over the life of your option. It does not guarantee that many jumps, however. It merely indicates that, on average, the number of jumps will be this number.

Option Type

There are size types of options you can choose from for hedging:

1. Vanilla European call.
2. Vanilla European put.
3. Vanilla American call.
4. Vanilla American put.
5. Knockout European call option.
6. Knockout European put option.

Push the "radio" button next to the Option Type of your choice. If you choose a barrier option, you will be prompted to enter the barrier level.

Additional Features

1. **Credit Limit.** You may add a credit limit by pushing the CREDIT LIMIT button and entering an amount for your credit limit.
2. **Randomize Volatility.** Ordinarily when you choose a volatility from the Basic Stock Features menu, this is the volatility the stock price path has. In real life, we do not know the "real" volatility of the stock path but only its historical volatility. By pressing the RANDOMIZE VOLATILITY button, the real volatility of the stock is hidden from you. The stock price path is generated using a volatility that might be different than the one you enter in the Volatility slider display box.

Playing the Game

Once you have chosen all of the desired features, it is time to play the SimuHedge game. To play, simply press PLAY GAME. After a brief pause, the Main Screen will appear, and you are ready to start playing the game. The Main Screen displays many important pieces of information (see Main Screen screen figure). The crucial points are described as follows:

1. There are three graphs along the top of the screen:

   a. *Stock price movements.* This is a record of the stock price movements over the life of the game. The graph will also contain a horizontal line displaying the strike price and a second horizontal line (in a different color) displaying the barrier level if the option is a barrier option. When you start the game, this graph is empty.

   b. *Close-up of stock price movements.* This is a record of the stock price movements since the last time you rebalanced your portfolio.

   c. *20-day volatility.* This displays the 20-day sliding volatility of the stock for the previous 20 days. Note that this is real-world volatility and will be different than the actual volatility. In other words, even if you choose a constant volatility stock price process, the 20-day sliding volatility will not appear at all constant.

2. When you hedge the option, you can take a position in the stock and in a riskless zero-coupon bond, which trades according to the current interest rate levels. The Current Position display shows you

    a. The number of shares of stock you own.

    b. The current value of the shares (assuming you have to buy at the ask price and sell at the bid price).

    c. The current par value of the bond you hold.

3. Below the current position display is the Current Market display. It shows the last bid and last ask price for the stock as well as the change in stock price from the previous tick and the current risk-free rate of interest. An important point to remark here is that *stocks trade with a tick size of* 1/8. This means that despite the fact that the theoretical stock price model (geometric Brownian motion) says stocks may trade at any prices whatsoever, in the trading simulation stocks trade as on a market.

4. To the right side of the screen are two columns of information about your option. The first column contains information about hedge parameters. All of these values are computed based on the current stock price and time to expiry and the volatility value you input into SimuHedge in the Hedge Vol slider display. The second column contains additional information about the option: the historical stock price volatility (as a guide to choosing a volatility to hedge the option with), number of days till expiry, strike price, number of shares, type of option and the style. Note: In SimuHedge you are always short the option.[1]

5. The volatility you want to compute the hedge parameter values with is your hedge volatility. You can input any number you wish here, and SimuHedge will automatically recompute the values. Note: The Hedge Vol display is automatically set to the historic volatility every time you rebalance your portfolio.

6. The Current P&L display keeps track of your current profit and loss. It has two entries:

    a. *Cash.* This is the amount of cash that has transacted to date. It does not include theoretical gains and losses due to changes in option value not realized in cash at this point.

    b. *Book.* This is the profit and loss to date, including gains and losses due to changes in theoretical option value. This book P&L is computed using the theoretical option value determined by the volatility you hedge with. Thus, every time you rebalance you have to choose a volatility. Note on book profits: When you initially sell the option, you sell it for some price and then set up a hedging portfolio. If the cost of your hedging portfolio is less than what you sold the option for, you will start off with a profit on the books.

7. Every time you rebalance your portfolio, the SimuHedge game moves you forward in time until a certain criterion (that you choose) is met. This criterion is determined by your current rebalancing strategy:

    a. *Days.* Wait a certain number of days and rebalance.

    b. *Stock.* Wait until the stock price moves more than a certain amount and rebalance.

---

[1]There are plans for a future release in which you can hedge a portfolio of different types of options in both long and short positions.

c. *Delta.* Wait until the option delta moves more than a certain amount and rebalance. You may choose a new rebalancing strategy each time you rebalance your portfolio.

8. The Stock Purchase display shows the number of shares you want to purchase and the cost of the purchase. (Compute as follows: If you are buying, you buy at the ask price; if you are selling, you sell at the bid price.) This display has two important features:

a. Every time you choose a Hedge Vol, it computes the number of shares you need to purchase to have your stock portfolio in balance.

b. It has a toggle button to the right of the slider that allows you to toggle between 0 and the correct number of shares to rebalance with.

9. The Bond Purchase display controls how many riskless zero-coupon bonds you want to trade. It displays two numbers: the current value of the bond (left side) and the par value of the bond (right side). It also has a "sticky button" to the right of the slider display that sets (and holds) the bond purchase amount to zero. Ordinarily when you rebalance your portfolio, SimuHedge displays the amount of bonds you need to purchase or sell to be in balance. If the sticky button is pressed, then when you rebalance, the bond purchase amount is set to zero. This feature is there so that you can delta hedge without buying or selling a bond.

10. Three control buttons—HEDGE, END, and SETUP—control the flow of the game; a fourth button, CONT, also can be used.

a. HEDGE puts on the hedge you have requested in the Stock and Bond Purchase boxes. It then updates the stock price path to the next time you need to rebalance (according to the strategy you have chosen), checks to see if an American option is exercised or a knockout option knocks out, and then updates your P&L.

b. END ends the game by not hedging any more. You do not put on a hedge, and you do not follow the strategy. You simply wait until the option is either exercised or expires.

c. SETUP brings the Setup screen forward. While in play, you may press the following from the Setup screen:

i. QUIT. Exit the game.

ii. NEW. Start a new game.

iii. UPDATE. You may change any of the input parameters concerning the stock price path (but not the option properties) during the life of the option and then press UPDATE.

d. If you want to continue with the same rebalancing strategy until the game has ended, press the CONT button. This allows you to more quickly answer some of the exercises that ask you to repetitively hedge in the same fashion.

Starting the Game

You may choose any settlement price you want for the option. This is the price you charge the client for the option, and this is the amount of cash that you receive when the transaction is made. Keep in mind several points:

- When the game starts, the settlement price is set to the historical volatility. That is, the historical stock price volatility is fed into the option pricing model, and this is used to determine an option's price.

- You may change the settlement price to anything you wish before you press HEDGE for the first time. After pressing HEDGE, the price is agreed upon, and you cannot change it.
- To change the settlement price, click in the Settled At: value box and change the value.

REVIEW QUESTIONS

In all of the following questions, we will refer to a stock S that follows a perfect geometric Brownian motion with volatility σ. Moreover, we assume interest rates are a constant r. You are required to use the hedging game to set up trading scenarios: you choose the volatility σ and interest rate r, time to expiration, stock price and strike price.

1. Set the Basic Stock Properties and Option Properties as follows:

$$
\begin{aligned}
\textbf{Stock price} &= \$100 \\
\textbf{Volatility} &= 15\% \\
\textbf{Risk-free rate} &= 10\% \\
\textbf{Dividend yield} &= 0\% \\
\textbf{Expiry} &= 30 \text{ days} \\
\textbf{Strike} &= \$100 \\
\textbf{Lot size} &= 1 \\
\textbf{Option} &= 1{,}000 \text{ shares}
\end{aligned}
$$

Sell the option at 15% volatility (instead of historical volatility). Now complete the following exercises:

a. Hedge the option using a 15% volatility over the life of the option, rebalancing once every day. What was your average P&L over 10 hedging runs?

b. Now do the same as in part a, but rebalance every time the delta moves by 0.01. What was your average P&L over 10 runs?

c. Now do the same as in part a, but rebalance every time the stock price moves by $0.50. What was your average P&L over 10 runs?

In general, as you increase rebalancing frequency, losses should decrease, that is, your total costs of hedging should be closer to the theoretical value of the option. Now, however, we will introduce transaction costs into the situation, by lowering liquidity.

Where transaction costs come from: The key point here is that with a bid-ask spread you have to buy stocks at a higher price than you can turn around and sell them for. In SimuHedge, we give a worst-case scenario and assume you can only hedge when placing market orders: You always buy at the offer and sell at the bid. In real markets you can do better than this by placing limit orders.

a. Redo the preceding exercises a, b, and c, but this time with a stock liquidity of 75%. What happens to your profits? Why?

b. Redo the exercises again, but this time with a stock liquidity of 50%. What happens to your profits? Why?

Try to draw some general conclusions about an optimal hedging strategy when there are transaction costs.

2. In this exercise we will overhedge the option by hedging with a volatility that is higher than the actual stock price volatility. We will still sell the option, however, for its historical volatility. This creates a problem: Initially we have to pay more for our hedge than we are receiving from the client. Do we make the profits up?

Set the Basic Stock properties and Option Properties as follows:

$$\begin{aligned}
\text{Stock price} &= \$100 \\
\text{Volatility} &= 15\% \\
\text{Risk-free rate} &= 10\% \\
\text{Dividend yield} &= 0\% \\
\text{Expiry} &= 30 \text{ days} \\
\text{Strike} &= \$100 \\
\text{Lot size} &= 1 \\
\text{Option} &= 1,000 \text{ shares}
\end{aligned}$$

Do the following exercises:

a. Sell the option at 16% volatility and hedge it at 16% volatility at every rebalancing.

i. What are your hedging setup costs? Are they the same or different from the settlement price? Why?

ii. Keep track of your total rebalancing costs. What are they?

b. Sell the option at 15% volatility, and hedge it at 5% volatility (i.e., at each rebalancing use 13.5% volatility). Answer the following questions as you hedge:

i. Your initial portfolio setup costs should be less than the settlement price, thus starting you off with a profit on the books. Do you "keep" this profit over the lifetime of the option? Is there a theoretical reason this would, in general, be impossible?

ii. The delta of an option is supposed to be rate of change of the option value with respect to the stock price. When you use 5% volatility to hedge on a 15% stock, what is typically the relationship between the delta reported by SimuHedge and the actual delta?

3. In this exercise we illustrate the effect of not knowing the correct volatility to hedge with, by using the Randomize Volatility feature in the Main Screen.

Set the Basic Stock Properties and Option Properties as follows:

$$\begin{aligned}
\text{Stock price} &= \$100 \\
\text{Volatility} &= 15\% \\
\text{Risk-free rate} &= 10\% \\
\text{Dividend yield} &= 0\% \\
\text{Expiry} &= 30 \text{ days} \\
\text{Strike} &= \$100 \\
\text{Lot size} &= 1 \\
\text{Option} &= 1,000 \text{ shares}
\end{aligned}$$

With the Randomize Volatility feature turned on, the actual stock price volatility is not known to you but is still constant. You will still obtain information about the historical volatility of the stock. It is up to you to determine

- How much to charge the client for the option.
- What volatility to use to hedge the option.
- How to make a profit.

Consider the following questions for discussion:

    a. In this exercise the stock price model still adheres to the Black-Scholes world, but it is typically more difficult to make a profit hedging the option. Why?

    b. The stock price volatility is constant, but its historical volatility jumps around quite a bit. Explain this.

    4. In this exercise we are going to study the approximate formula for the delta we studied in *Black-Scholes and Beyond* (see pp. 135–38). Our main purpose is to show why Black-Scholes fails when you introduce random (stochastic) volatility into the stock price model.

    Set the Basic Stock Properties and Option Properties as follows:

$$\begin{aligned}
\textbf{Stock price} &= \$100\\
\textbf{Volatility} &= 15\%\\
\textbf{Risk-free rate} &= 0\%\\
\textbf{Dividend yield} &= 0\%\\
\textbf{Expiry} &= 30 \text{ days}\\
\textbf{Strike} &= \$100\\
\textbf{Lot size} &= 1\\
\textbf{Option} &= 1{,}000 \text{ shares}
\end{aligned}$$

Because we set the risk-free rate to 0, the approximate formula for the delta now reads

$$\Delta = \frac{C_{t_1} - C_{t_0}}{S_{t_1} - S_{t_0}}$$

Compute the approximate formula for the delta by using SimuHedge as follows:

    a. After setting the input parameters to the values given, go to the Main Screen and set the Hedging Volatility to 15%.

    b. Set the Hedging Strategy to 0.10 day (this is the minimum resolution of the hedging game).

    c. Record the current stock price (S_{t_0}), the current option value (C_{t_0}), and delta (Δ). Press HEDGE.

    d. Record the new stock price (S_{t_1}), and new option value (C_{t_1}), and compute

$$\frac{C_{t_1} - C_{t_0}}{S_{t_1} - S_{t_0}}$$

Compare this with the value of Δ recorded in the part c. Do this for several iterations of the stock price movement. What conclusions can you draw?

    e. Do you think the fact that stock prices trade at one-eighth intervals diminishes the effectiveness of the approximate formula for the delta?

f. Now set the strategy to 1 day instead of 0.1 day, and perform the exercises a through d again. How does the approximate formula for the Δ hold up now?

g. Repeat the exercise f for a five-day rebalancing strategy. What happens? What are some theoretical reasons the approximate formula begins to break down? (Hint: Consider some other hedge parameters.)

If you set all of the parameters correctly, you should have discovered that for small changes in time, the approximate formula is very good indeed. Now we are going to explore the effect of using the wrong volatility on the approximate formula for the delta. Complete the following exercises, keeping the inputs to the hedging game the same as in the previous exercise:

a. Redo the preceding exercises, but this time compute the delta of the option, and rebalance with a volatilities of 16%, 18%, and 20%. How does the value of the "theoretical" delta (at 16%, 18%, and 20%) compare with the value of the "approximate" delta?

b. Restart the SimuHedge game, but this time add stochastic volatility as follows:

   i. Set the mean volatility to 15%.

   ii. Set the reversion strength to 2.

Redo the computation of the approximate delta. How does stochasticity of volatility affect the accuracy of the approximate formula for the delta?

c. What theoretical reasons explain the lack of success of the approximate formula for the delta? (Hint: See *Black-Scholes and Beyond,* p. 137.)

Using *Black-Scholes and Beyond Interactive Toolkit* Software

WHAT IS THE *BLACK-SCHOLES AND BEYOND INTERACTIVE TOOLKIT* SOFTWARE?

The *Black-Scholes and Beyond Interactive Toolkit* is a specially compiled version of the MAT-LAB software package designed for Irwin Professional Publishing. It consists of four programs:

1. The Options Calculator, by Neil A. Chriss.
2. The SimuHedge Hedging Game, by Neil A. Chriss.
3. The Random Number Tool, by The Mathworks.
4. The Probability Distribution Tool, by The Mathworks.

The Options Calculator and SimuHedge were developed especially for use with *Black-Scholes and Beyond* and the *Black-Scholes and Beyond Interactive Toolkit* by the author. In addition to these programs, your software includes a demonstration version of MATLAB. If you know how to use MATLAB, then from the ">>" prompt you may use most of the commands familiar to you in MATLAB.[1] You can use the demonstration version of MATLAB as a desktop calculator and for simple plotting, but its main purpose is to use the numeric and graphics capabilities of MATLAB to run the Options Calculator and SimuHedge game.

Installing the *Black-Scholes and Beyond Interactive Toolkit* software

The *Black-Scholes and Beyond Interactive Toolkit* comes with two diskettes bound in the back.

The Main Screen

When you run the *Black-Scholes and Beyond Interactive Toolkit* software package, a main screen will pop up with four options:

1. Options Calculator.
2. SimuHedge Hedging Game.
3. Random Number Tool.
4. Probability Distribution Tool.

Proceed by pressing any of the buttons.

---

[1] Some restrictions apply. For information on how to get more out of your Demo Version of MATLAB, contact The Mathworks.

We now give a comprehensive reference guide to the *Black-Scholes and Beyond Interactive Toolkit* Options Calculator. This reference is valid for Toolkit version 1.2 only. The version number may be found in the title of the Options Calculator screen.

BASIC GRAPHICAL USER INTERFACE CONCEPTS

The following is a glossary of basic "point-and-click" concepts used throughout without comment. These are not examples of how to use the calculator but rather a description of the basic components that make up the calculator.

There are several components to the calculator screen:

- **The mouse pointer.** The mouse pointer is the fundamental object with which you control the calculator. You move the mouse pointer by sliding your mouse in the desired direction.

- **The menu bar.** At the top of the screen there is a menu bar with the following labels: "Main," "Configuration," "Implied Trees," and "Implied Volatility." You may select items from the menus by moving the mouse pointer over the desired item and clicking the left mouse button.

- **Pull-down menus.** There are many pull-down menus on the screen. Across the top row are three labeled as follows: "Option Type," "Evaluation Method," and "Underlying Type." Below each is a description of the current item. For example, when you start up the calculator, the current item for the "Option Type" menu is always Vanilla Call. To change the current type, move the mouse pointer over the menu you wish to change, and press the left mouse button. A list of options will appear. Drag the mouse pointer to the desired menu item and release. The new menu item should appear.

- **Slider displays.** Slider displays have three components: slider name display, slider value box, and slider. The slider is, in turn, broken into three parts: slider left-arrow, slider right-arrow, and slider bar.

    Slider displays are the fundamental way to enter and adjust values relevant to option pricing. They allow you to quickly adjust values by pressing slider buttons, or enter precise values by typing directly into the Slider Value.

    To change a Slider Display value you may do one of the following:

    a. Press the left slider arrow to lower the current value. Depending on the slider's range of values, the Slider Value box will change a certain amount.

    b. Press the right slider arrow to raise the current value. Depending on the slider's range of values, the Slider Value box will change a certain amount.

    c. Slide the slider bar to a new position.

    d. Move the mouse pointer over the Slider Display box and click the left mouse button. A cursor will appear, and you can delete the old value and enter a new value. If you hit RETURN, the slider bar will move to the appropriate position.

- **Pushbuttons.** There are many displays in the calculator that look like commands, such as PLOT X-Z or ENTER DIV'DS. Such buttons can be "pressed" to do their task by moving the mouse pointer over them and pressing the left mouse button. If the button is a pushbutton, it will change colors slightly so that you know it is being activated. When you release it, it will perform the desired task.

THE OPTIONS CALCULATOR SCREENS

The details of using the Options Calculator are contained in the various sections of this book. This section is a guide to the screens attached to the Options Calculator. The main components of the Options Calculator are as follows:

1. Options Calculator Version 1.2 Main Screen.
2. Tree Display.
3. 2-d Option Graph Screen.
4. 3-d Option Graph.
5. Smile Input Screen.
6. Dividend Entry Screen.

See the next few pages for details on these screens.

BUILDING VERY LARGE TREES USING THE OPTIONS CALCULATOR: IMPACT ON PERFORMANCE

The performance of your Options Calculator depends on the configuration of your machine. The more dynamic random access memory (RAM) your machine possesses, the more efficiently your Options Calculator will run.

The Options Calculator sets no predefined limits on the size trees you can build, but building large trees can tie up a lot of memory and slow down performance. If you try to build a tree that exceeds the current memory capacity of your machine, you will get an "Out of Memory" error in the MATLAB work area. Should this happen, you may proceed in one of two ways:

1. *Try this first:* From the Options Calculator main screen, pull down the "Main" menu and choose the Free Memory menu item. This will clear all trees in the system, including Implied Volatility trees.

2. *More drastic:* If the first attempt fails, the next thing you may try is to type RESTART from the MATLAB work area. This will free up all of the memory MATLAB is using, clear all graphic screens, and start the session over. Of course, any work you were doing in the calculator will be lost.

Sometimes, performance of the Options Calculator can become sluggish if a lot of large trees are being stored in memory. You may free up some of this memory by using the Free Memory menu item from the "Main" menu.

THE SIMUHEDGE SCREENS

There are three screens in the SimuHedge game:

1. SimuHedge Main Screen.
2. SimuHedge Setup Screen.
3. SimuHedge Summary Screen.

See the next few pages for details on these screens.

GRAPHICS CAPABILITIES

The *Black-Scholes and Beyond Interactive Toolkit* software package supports sophisticated two- and three-dimensional graphics capabilities, including the following:

1. Zoom in and out of all two-dimensional graphs:

   a. Click the left mouse button anywhere on a two-dimensional graph (in either the Options Calculator or the SimuHedge game) and zoom in 2×. Click the right mouse button anywhere on any of the graphs and zoom out 2×.

   b. Hold down the left mouse button, and draw a box around the portion of the graph you want to enlarge. Release the mouse button, and see that portion enlarged.

   c. Changing the graph resolution (Options Calculator only): You may change the fineness of the graphing by entering the "Graph Resolution" menu in the "Configuration" pull-down menu in the Options Calculator main screen. Fine resolution has the most detail for closeup viewing of graphs but takes the longest to compute.

2. Grab-and-go three-dimensional rotation: Rotate any three-dimensional graph by moving the mouse pointer over the graph and holding down the left mouse button. A box frame will appear, and moving the mouse button will rotate the frame. Remember to always keep the X at the bottom of the box for proper orientation.

These capabilities were provided by The Mathworks Inc. as part of the MATLAB software package.

TROUBLESHOOTING GUIDE TO THE OPTIONS CALCULATOR

Q. What do I do if I press the ENTER DIV'DS button and nothing happens?

A. This probably means the Enter Dividend screen is already open but hidden behind another screen. The Options Calculator will not allow you to have two Enter Dividend screens open simultaneously; therefore, you should find the open Enter Dividend screen and use that.

Q. How does the Calculator determine the range in which to plot the X-axis in two-dimensional plotting?

A. Say you choose Stock Price as your X-axis value. The computer first looks at the current stock price in the Stock Price slider display. Then it chooses a range from 40% to 140% of the current stock price value.

If the X-axis value is Number of Periods, the stock samples from 3 to 60 periods for the graph at a rate of once per four periods, and then from 63 to 100 periods at a rate of once per six periods.

Q. If there are dates in my dividend schedule beyond the option expiry, will they be computed in the Black-Scholes formula?

A. No. When you compute the value of an option, only the ex-dividend dates relevant for that option's expiry are used.

Q. When I display binomial trees, can I have more than one type of tree open at once? For example, can I have the stock price tree and the option price tree open at the same time?

A. Yes, you can have as many different types of trees displayed as you like.

Q. When you put a dividend schedule into the system, the ex-dividend dates do not necessarily coincide with the nodes of the binomial trees we build. How does the Calculator build trees with lumpy dividends in this case?

A. The tree uses an approximation technique. When the Calculator builds the tree, it first determines the times of each node. Then, for each ex-dividend date, it determines the node nearest to that date. Next, it adjusts the value of the dividend payment for the time value between the actual ex-dividend date and the date of the node.

Q. The user has a choice between two- and four-digit output precision. What kind of precision do we have for inputs?

A. Input precision is only limited by the size of MATLAB's internal computational precision. To enter high-precision input variables, type directly into the slider display box of the desired input parameter.

Q. Sometimes when I press IMPLIED VOLATILITY I have the evaluation method set to something other than analytic, yet I still get an implied volatility. Is the Options Calculator producing a different type of implied volatility?

A. No. When you press the IMPLIED VOLATILITY button, the Calculator checks to see if the evaluation method is set to analytic. If it is not, then the calculator will automatically set the method to analytic.

Q. When I am entering a volatility smile, what happens if I try to build a tree but the expiries or strikes are not in ascending order?

A. When you try to build an implied volatility tree, the Options Calculator automatically checks to see if the expiries and strikes are in order and automatically orders them before trying to build the tree.

Q. If there is currently an implied volatility tree in the system and I use it to evaluate an option, what happens if the number of periods currently selected in the Periods slider display does not equal the number of periods in the tree. Does the Options Calculator build a new tree? What about if the stock price is set differently than the current stock price of the implied volatility tree?

A. No. The Options Calculator will continue to use the tree in the system until you build a new tree from the Smile Input screen (which you can get to by pressing BUILD TREE or VIEW/EDIT SMILE). When you press EVALUATE OPTION, the Calculator computes how big the current implied volatility tree is and sets the Periods slider display to that number.

Q. If the current implied volatility tree is one year in duration and I try to price an option on it with a two-year expiry, what happens?

A. The Options Calculator will display an error box. When you use the Options Calculator to price an option on an implied tree, the Calculator checks to make sure the length expiry time of the option is less than the duration of the implied volatility tree currently in the system.

Q. If I build an implied volatility tree and then price options with other evaluation methods, can I return to the implied volatility tree method and price more options, or do I have to build a new tree?

A. You do not have to build a new tree. As long as you do not free memory with the Free Memory menu option, all trees that you create remain in the system.

Q. Does the Dividend Yield slider have anything to do with the implied volatility model?

A. No. The installation of the implied volatility model here only uses lumpy dividends.

Q. How are dividends handled with implied volatility trees?

A. When you press BUILD TREE from the Smile Input screen, the Options Calculator records the current set of lumpy dividends in the system. Whenever you return to the evaluation method menu and change the implied volatility to price an option, this set of dividends replaces the current set. When you return to evaluate another set of options, the old set is put back. In this way the system carries two sets of lumpy dividends: one for the implied tree and one for all other methods. When you evaluate an option using a given method, the relevant set of dividends is activated. Thus, you can view the set of lumpy dividends for the current implied tree by first evaluating an option with the implied tree and then viewing the current set of lumpy dividends.

Q. After building an implied volatility tree, can I price options on the tree of expirations not equal to the duration of the tree?

A. Yes, as long as the expiration is less than the duration of the tree. For example, if you build a one-year implied volatility tree, you can price any option on that tree with an expiration of less than one year. The only caveat here is that as a result of the coarseness of the tree, the expiration you want may not be represented on the tree. The Options Calculator will inform you of what expiration and number of periods were used to price the option.

Q. When I evaluate an option using an implied tree, vega is not computed. Why?

A. There is no notion of vega for pricing on implied volatility trees. The notion of vega only makes sense when a single volatility parameter is an input to an option volatility model (remember, vega is the rate of change of option value with respect to volatility). An implied tree model takes an entire surface of volatilities as an input.

Q. When I set the Expiry Units to years, the slider for expiry will not move past one year. Sometimes I want to enter times such as 0.2 year. Can I do this?

A. Yes. Simply move the mouse pointer to the window that displays the expiry, and click the left mouse button. Now directly enter whatever value you wish.

Q. In what units is theta computed?

A. Theta is change in option price per unit change in time, where the units are specified by the "Units" submenu of the "Configuration" menu. For example, if the units are set to Weeks, then theta will represent change in option value per week.

Q. Sometimes the Options Calculator's performance almost grinds to a halt. Why does this happen, and is there anything I can do about it?

A. Storing large binomial trees in the Options Calculator is the main reason performance slows down significantly. You may free up this memory by selecting the "Free memory" menu item from the "Main" menu.

Using the *Black-Scholes and Beyond Interactive Toolkit* with the Options Calculator

This section collects together some standard notations used throughout the book.

INDEX OF NOTATION

Certain notation is used throughout this book, and we explain here what the notation is and how it is used. The following notation remains consistent throughout this book:

S = Stock price
K = Strike price
T = time to expiry
σ = annualized volatility
r = risk-free interest rate
q = annual continuous dividend yield
n = number of time periods in a binomial tree

Notation and the Options Pricing Calculator

We call the preceding notation the standard inputs to option pricing models (S, K, T, σ, r, q, and sometimes n). Each standard input has a corresponding slider display in the Options Pricing calculator. Many exercises in this book explicitly require you to set the standard input values in the slider displays. Thus, an exercise might require you to set the standard inputs as follows:

S = \$100
K = \$100
T = 1 year
σ = 15%
r = 10%
q = 0%

Explicitly this means to first set the stock price slider display to \$100, then set the strike price slider display to \$100, etc.

Using the MATLAB Command Window

Now that you have used the toolkit, try using some MATLAB functions in the MATLAB Command Window.

To restore the Main Map window, type *fexpemap* in the Command Window.

When you are finished with the MATLAB Command window, type **EXIT** or pull down the "**File**" menu and click **EXIT MATLAB.**

MATLAB COMMANDS

First, create a simple row vector, called a, that has nine elements. Separate the numbers with spaces.

$$>> a = [1\ 2\ 3\ 4\ 6\ 4\ 3\ 4\ 5]$$

Now add two to each element of a, and store the result in a new vector b. Note that MATLAB requires no special handling of vector or matrix math.

$$b = a + 2$$

Creating graphs in MATLAB is as easy as one command. To plot the result of our vector addition:

$$>> \text{plot(b)}$$
$$>> \text{grid}$$
$$>> \text{title('The First Graph')}$$

The Plot command graphs the elements of b. The Grid statement adds the grid, and the Title statement adds the title.

In the figure window, pull down the "**File**" menu and click **CLOSE** to close the window.

MATLAB truly excels in matrix computation. Creating a matrix is as easy as creating a vector; just use semicolons (;) to separate the rows of a matrix. Pay attention to case: A and a are different variables:

$$>> A = [1\ 2\ 0;\ 2\ 5 - 1;\ 4\ 10 - 1]$$

Now find the transpose of the matrix A:

$$>> B = A'$$

Now multiply the two matrices. Note again that MATLAB doesn't make you deal with matrices as a collection of numbers. MATLAB knows when you are dealing with matrices and adjusts calculations accordingly.

$$>> C = A * B$$

    Instead of doing matrix multiplication, you can do element-by-element multiplication using the period (.) operator:

$$>> C = A .* B$$

To find the inverse of a matrix:

$$>> X = \text{inv}(A)$$

Now illustrate the fact that a matrix times its inverse is the identity matrix.

$$>> I = \text{inv}(A) * A$$

At any time, you can get a listing of the variables stored in the MATLAB workspace by typing the Who or Whos command.

$$>> \text{whos}$$

You can also see the current value of a particular variable by typing its name.

$$>> A$$